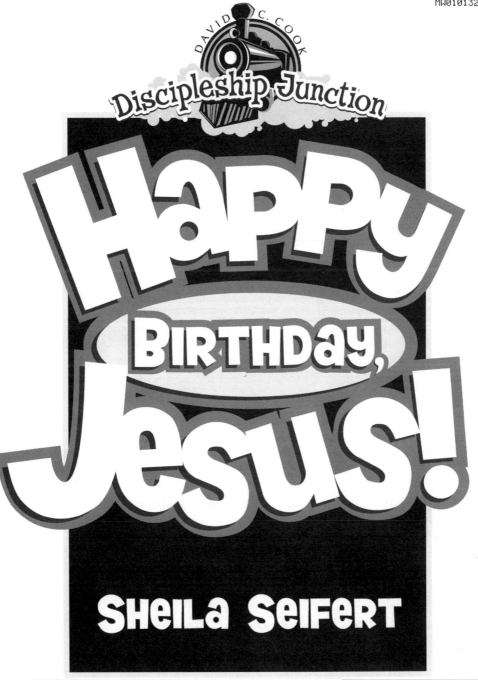

DAVID C. COOK
Discipleship Junction

Happy BIRTHDAY, Jesus!

SHEILA SEIFERT

NEXGEN®

Building the New Generation of Believers

COOK COMMUNICATIONS MINISTRIES
Colorado Springs, Colorado • Paris, Ontario
KINGSWAY COMMUNICATIONS LTD
Eastbourne, England

NexGen® is an imprint of
Cook Communications Ministries
Colorado Springs, CO 80918
Cook Communications, Paris, Ontario
Kingsway Communications, Eastbourne, England

HAPPY BIRTHDAY, JESUS!
© 2007 by Cook Communications Ministries

Cover Design: BMB Design
Cover Illustration: BMB Design/Ryan Putnam
Interior Design: TrueBlue Design/Sandy Flewelling
Interior Illustrations: Aline Heiser

First Printing 2007
Printed in the United States of America

1 2 3 4 5 6 7 8 9 10

ISBN 978-0-7814-4511-5   105278

Table of Contents

WELCOME TO DISCIPLESHIP JUNCTION!

Discipleship Junction is an all-new program that harnesses the power of *FUN* to build young disciples through interaction with Bible truth and with each other.

A complete, multi-age children's ministry program, *Discipleship Junction* is packed full of interactive stories and drama, Scripture memory, and themed snacks and activities that will engage every child! It's guaranteed effective because its principles and methods of instruction are *teacher-tested* and *kid-approved!*

Intensive student-teacher interaction within a learning community that is relational and supportive makes *Discipleship Junction* an ideal program for including children with disabilities. Hands-on learning activities are easily adapted to include all students. For more ideas about inclusion, an excellent resource is *Let All the Children Come to Me* by MaLesa Breeding, Ed.D., Dana Hood, Ph.D., and Jerry Whitworth, Ed.D., (Colorado Springs: Cook Communications Ministries, 2006).

PUTTING THE PIECES TOGETHER

Get Set! We know you're busy, so we provide a list of materials and what you'll need to do to prepare for your lesson. You'll also need a photocopy machine and some basic classroom supplies: paper, pencils, markers, butcher paper, scissors, glue, and index cards. When you see this icon ⏲ allow a little extra prep time.

Kids love to dress up! Many of our Bible lessons use costume props from the *Bible time dress-up box*. This can be as simple as a box of items you gather from around the house or purchase inexpensively from a second-hand store. It should include: fake beards, an assortment of headcloths and robes or tunics, modern-day men's and women's clothes, props for worship dancers, and pretend microphones.

Tickets Please! *(10 minutes)* Each week begins with an activity option to involve children while others are being dropped off by parents.

■ The *Welcome Time Activity* will excite children's interest and help them connect with the Bible Truth for the week.

All Aboard for Bible Truth! *(20 minutes)* Whole group, interactive Bible lessons invite students ages 6–11 to participate in the entire lesson. In *Happy Birthday, Jesus!*, kids will look for answers to the questions, "Who is Jesus?" and "Why did he come?" They'll marvel at the prophecies that foretold the coming of the Messiah, be there to see how God announces his son, and finally finish the program with a celebration of the Savior's birth! Whether building gumdrop pyramids or interviewing John the Baptist, kids will always be engaged in exciting, hands-on lessons.

■ Pre- and post-lesson discussion times encourage children to tie their own life experiences to the week's Bible Truth.

■ *Use the Clues!* Practice is an important part of learning, and helps us move information from short-term to long-term memory. *Happy Birthday, Jesus!* uses the theme of a celebration—complete with a giant cake—to help kids practice and apply what they learn. Every week one door of the Celebration Calendar is opened to reveal a clue behind the door. In the weeks that follow, kids are repeatedly challenged to remember the Bible truth connected with each clue. These "memory hooks" help the Bible truth stick with kids for a long time to come.

Bible Memory Waypoint *(5 minutes)*. Toe tappin' and finger snappin' . . . there's nothing like the power of *FUN* to motivate children. Movement, rhythm, and role-play make it easy for kids to hide God's Word in their hearts (Psalm 119:11).

Prayer Station (15 minutes). Small-group prayer time for children. Wow! What an idea! Children break into small groups of three to five with an adult helper—we call them StationMasters. Using reproducible instruction cards, adults guide children to explore and practice new prayer skills. Together they'll share concerns, praise God, and practice the four activities of prayer: *praise, ask, confess, give thanks.*

(Optional) **Snack Stop and Activities** (10 minutes). Tied to the theme of the lesson, you have options for snacks and activities in which lesson truths are practiced and shared. Look for the throttle icon which shows the level of mess, energy, or noise required for the activity!

On the Fast Track! Reproducible take-home pages invite families to interact in and through fun activities and Bible memory.

Are you looking for an additional way to motivate young learners? *Discipleship Junction* includes an optional incentive program which rewards students for completing take-home pages. Children return a signed *Fast Track!* Ticket and choose a prize from the treasure box. If you have a new student, you might welcome that child with the choice of a treasure too! Simply cover and decorate a large shoebox. Fill with inexpensive items such as you might find at a party store.

HOW TO GET STARTED

1. ***Begin by recruiting StationMasters***—adult helpers who will guide children through the process of praying in small groups. Don't have enough adult volunteers? How about recruiting middle- or high-schoolers to shepherd a group? Also consider enlisting a few faithful prayer partners who will commit to praying for your class weekly.

   Plan to have a brief training session with your volunteers in which you'll explain how to use the imPACT model of prayer. Each week you'll give the StationMasters a reproducible instruction card with the day's prayer theme and prayer suggestions to use with children in a small group.

2. ***Set up your room.*** You'll need a big area for your large-group Bible teaching time. You'll also need to identify spaces for each of your small prayer groups. Don't forget that moving chairs and tables or moving groups to a hallway is always an option. And children are willing helpers!

3. ***Photocopy reproducible letters*** (see Resources) to StationMasters and parents. Mail these two or three weeks before you begin your children's ministry program.

4. ***Photocopy*** **On the Fast Track!** pages for each child, and *StationMaster Cards* for each adult helper. If you choose, make copies of the reproducibles for all the lessons ahead of time. This can save a last-minute scramble when time is tight!

5. ***Make your Celebration Calendar.*** Make a 3' or 4' tall enlargement of the Celebration Calendar. You can do this by making a photocopy of the pattern (see Resources) on transparency film and projecting it onto a wall with an overhead projector. Then, trace the outline on a large piece of poster board taped to the wall. Cut out the cake *and* three sides of each door where indicated. Number the doors 1–13, one for each lesson. (Kids will open one door each week in class, like an Advent calendar.) Mount the cake cutout on another poster board the same size. Then, glue a picture (see Resources) behind each door, being careful to match the numbers. Finally, add some color and mount it on the wall in your lesson area.

6. ***Gather and prepare your materials,*** set out your snacks, and you are ready to roll. So . . . **FULL SPEED AHEAD! ALL ABOARD FOR DISCIPLESHIP JUNCTION!**

LESSON ONE: Adam and Eve and Me?

Memory Verse:

I am not ashamed of the gospel, because it is the power of God for the salvation of everyone who believes (Romans 1:16).

*Early elementary verse in **bold** type.*

Bible Basis:

Genesis 1:26–30; 2:8–17; 3:1–6, 14–15

Bible Truth:

Every person needs a Savior.

You Will Need:

- ☐ Celebration Calendar
- ☐ 1 poster board
- ☐ play dough
- ☐ beanbag or soft ball
- ☐ construction paper in a variety of "fruit colors"
- ☐ Bibles
- ☐ brown construction or butcher paper
- ☐ *On the Fast Track! #1* take-home paper
- ☐ *StationMaster Card #1*
- ☐ *(optional)* treasure box
- ☐ *(optional)* snack: napkins, gingerbread people cookies, frosting, plastic knives, cookie decorations
- ☐ *(optional)* Activity #2: play dough

 When you see this icon, it means preparation will take more than five minutes.

GET SET!

(Lesson Preparation)

- ■ Print today's Bible memory verse on a poster board:
  I am not ashamed of the gospel, because it is the power of God for the salvation of everyone who believes (Romans 1:16).
- ■ Cut out various 8" fruit shapes from colored construction paper. Write one or two words from the memory verse on each shape.
- ■ Make a copy of *On the Fast Track! #1* take-home paper for each child.
- ■ Make a copy of *StationMaster Card #1* for each helper.
- ■ Set out the Celebration Calendar and *(optional)* treasure box.
- ■ Set up snack and outside play activities if you include these items in your children's ministry.
- ■ Place play dough on tables for the Welcome Time Activity.
- ■ Cut out a wall-size tree trunk with branches from brown construction or butcher paper and attach it to the wall in your story area. You may draw this freehand or use the family tree as a template (see Resources).
- ■ Cut out five 8" apple shapes from construction paper. Print one of the following Bible references and questions on each one:

  1. Genesis 1:26–27   What else did God make? What was he like?
  2. Genesis 1:28   What was their job?
  3. Genesis 1:29–30   What did they eat?
  4. Genesis 2:8-9, 15   Where did they live?
  5. Genesis 2:16–17   What did God tell them?

Play Dough Recipe

- 2 c. flour
- 1 c. salt
- 4 T. cream of tartar
- 1 pkg. unsweetened powdered drink mix for scent and color
- 2 c. warm water
- 2 T. cooking oil

Stir over medium heat until mixture pulls away from sides to form a ball. Store in airtight container. *(for 8 to 10 children)*

TICKETS PLEASE!
(Welcome and Bible Connection)

- **Objective:** *To excite their interest and connect their own life experiences with the Bible Truth, children will make play dough people.*

Welcome Time Activity: Clay Creations

- **Materials:** *play dough*

As children arrive, direct them to the table with play dough. Encourage them to make as many people as possible.

Sharing Time and Bible Connection

When everyone has arrived, call children to the lesson area and welcome them. **You did a great job of making play dough people. It looks like you've made an entire city of them!** As you talk, give every child the opportunity to say something.

- **If you really could make a person, someone who would be your friend, what would you make that person like?**
- **What are your real friends like?**
- **Do they always make good choices?**
- **What would you do if your friend made a bad choice?**

Making people out of play dough is easy. Making real people is impossible for us. Only God can do that. He made every single thing in the world—even us! When God made people, he wanted to have a friendship with them. But after he made them, they had a problem. Today we're going to get into small groups and see what the Bible says happened.

ALL ABOARD FOR BIBLE TRUTH Genesis 1:26–30; 2:8–17; 3:1–6, 14–15
(Bible Discover and Learn Time)

■ **Objective:** *Children will study Genesis 1:26–30; 2:8–17; and 3:1–6, 14–15 and hear how humans sinned against God after he created them.*

■ **Materials:** *Bibles, five 8" paper apples with Scripture references, tree trunk on wall, markers, tape*

Divide your class into five multi-age groups of three to five kids. Be sure you have a confident reader in each group. Give each group a Bible and an apple with a reference on it and show them where to find Genesis. Have groups look up and read the apple verses together. Then, write the answer to their question on the apple and be ready to share it with the rest of the class. Allow a few minutes to complete this task, then gather children in the story area again.

What are some of the things God made when he created the world? Accept responses, then ask Group 1 to read their apple questions and answers to the class. Affirm their answers: **Yes! God made man in his image.** Have the group tape the apple onto a tree branch. **When God created people, like you and me, he looked forward to being friends with us. Those first two people were close friends with God. Their names were Adam and Eve. God gave them work to do.** Have Group 2 read their question and answer, then tape the apple to a branch. **That's right, God gave Adam and Eve the job of taking care of the birds, fish, and animals. God gave his new people everything they needed—food and a wonderful place to live.** Ask Group 3 to share and tape up the apple. **What kinds of fruit do you think were there?** Accept children's suggestions, then ask Group 4 to share. **The garden was a beautiful place. Adam and Eve took care of it and the animals. They were good friends with God, and they were very happy. God gave Adam and Eve some instructions.** Ask Group 5 to share, then tape up their apple. **So, Adam and Eve could climb a tree to pick coconuts or oranges. They could pull a banana from a banana plant or pluck strawberries from the ground. They could eat anything and everything, except one thing.** Dramatic pause. **What was that?** Let children respond. **Yes, God said not to eat from the tree of the knowledge of good and evil.**

One day a tricky serpent talked to Eve. Use a loud whisper. **"Did God really say you must not eat from any tree in the garden?"**

"Oh no," Eve answered. "We can eat from any tree but one. God said that if we eat the fruit from it, we will die."

Use a sneaky voice. **"You won't die," said the serpent. "Once you eat from this tree, your eyes will be opened, and you will be as wise as God."**

Oh, that fruit on the forbidden tree looked so good! Eve decided to disobey God. She picked off a fruit and ate some. What's worse, she gave some to Adam too! As soon as they ate it, they knew something was wrong. They felt miserable. They had disobeyed God. Their choice to disobey God was the first sin, and it was a bad thing.

God knew what Adam and Eve had done. God was sad, too. He wanted to be Adam and Eve's closest friend, but now their sin was in the way. Sin made a mess of God's beautiful world.

And you know what? You and I have also done wrong. We've all disobeyed God in some way and are trapped by sin too.

But there's good news! God still wants to be friends with people. He saw that <u>people needed to be saved from their sin</u>. God made a plan to free Adam and Eve, and all the people after them, from sin. He would send someone to save us!

God's plan didn't happen right away. It was still a long way off. Next week we'll find out more about the Savior God promised to send!

Use the Clues!
(Bible Review)

- **Materials:** *beanbag or soft ball*

Okay, let's see what you remember. For this review game, toss a beanbag to a child and ask a question about the Bible story. If they answer correctly, they get to toss the bag to another student, who will then answer a question. If the child can't answer correctly, he tosses the bag back to you and you toss it to another student.

- **What was life like for the first two people, Adam and Eve?** (they lived in a garden, they were happy and safe, God was their friend)
- **What one rule did God give Adam and Eve?** (not to eat the fruit from the tree of the knowledge of good and evil)

- **How was Eve tempted to disobey God?** (a serpent lied to her)
- **What happened when Eve and Adam chose to go disobey God?** (they felt miserable, they knew they had done wrong, they lost their close friendship with God)
- **What is the problem you and I have that started with Adam and Eve?** (we all sin, we need a Savior)

Show the children the Celebration Calendar and explain that each week, the class will open one door to find a symbol from that Bible lesson. The symbol will help them remember what they learned from the Bible that week. **What do you think is behind the door for today?** Let children call out their guesses of the picture under today's door. Choose a child to open door #1. **When you see the picture of this tree, remember that it shows us we all need a Savior.**

BIBLE MEMORY WAYPOINT   Romans 1:16
(Scripture Memory)

- **Objective:** *Children will hide God's Word in their hearts for guidance, protection, and encouragement.*
- **Materials:** *construction paper fruit shapes with verse words*

I am not ashamed of the gospel, because it is the power of God for the salvation of everyone who believes (Romans 1:16).

Read this week's memory verse from the poster and let the children echo you. Practice the verse by handing out the fruit shapes with the verse words on them. Have children line up so the verse is in the correct order. Walk around the line and have each child say the word(s) he or she is holding when you pass. Then have the whole group repeat the verse in unison. Scramble the fruit and play again.

PRAYER STATION

- **Objective:** *Children will explore and practice prayer for themselves in small groups.*
- **Materials:** *copies of* StationMaster Card #1 *for each adult or teen helper*

Break into small groups of three to five children. Assign a teen or adult helper to each small group and give each helper a copy of *StationMaster Card #1* (see Resources) with ideas for group discussion and prayer.

SNACK STOP: IN HIS IMAGE (Optional)

If you plan to provide a snack, this is an ideal time to serve it.

- **Materials:** *napkins, gingerbread people cookies, frosting, plastic knives, cookie decorations*

Give each child a plastic knife, napkin, and gingerbread person. Allow children to decorate their gingerbread person to look like themselves. As they decorate, talk about how we are made in God's image—having feelings, a spirit, wanting to have relationships with others. Talk about how each person has sinned and needs a Savior. Once the cookies are decorated, children can eat them.

Note: Always be aware of children with food allergies and have another option on hand if necessary.

APPLICATION

■ **Objective:** *Children will have opportunities to show how the lesson works in their own lives through activities and take-home papers.*

Some children's ministries may allow children to play outside at this point. If yours does not, choose one of the following activities.

Fruit Basket Upset

Use the fruit concept to play a game that reviews the memory verse. Choose three or more kinds of fruit, depending on the size of your class. Go around the room and whisper one of the three types in each child's ear, trying to assign an equal number of children to each fruit type. After all have been assigned, call out an action for the children to do (hop on one foot, walk backward, twirl in place, crab walk, skip, etc.) After 10 seconds call out, "fruit basket upset!" At that signal, children should find others who have the same fruit name and gather together. The group that is gathered first must say the memory verse in unison before being declared the winner. Assign new types of fruit—use non-ordinary types too, such as kiwi, pineapple, cherries, figs, and kumquats—and play again. Make sure the actions the children do fit the size of the playing area and the number of players.

Play Dough Eden

■ **Materials:** *play dough*

Have children cluster in small groups. Distribute play dough and have each group cooperatively design a replica of the Garden of Eden. They can make the people, animals, plants, birds, serpent, tree of the knowledge of good and evil, etc.

ON THE FAST TRACK! *(Take-Home Papers)*

Introduce the treasure box: **This treasure box will be here every week. When you take your *On the Fast Track!* paper home each week and do the activities, your parents can sign the ticket to show that you finished the work. Bring the signed ticket back to get a prize from the treasure box!** Distribute the take-home papers just before children leave.

LESSON TWO: God Promises a Savior

Memory Verse:

And we have seen and testify that **the Father has sent his Son to be the Savior of the world (1 John 4:14).**

*Early elementary verse in **bold** type.*

Bible Basis:

Genesis 17, 21

Bible Truth:

God promises Abraham the Savior would come from his family.

You Will Need:

- ☐ Celebration Calendar (with all doors closed again)
- ☐ 1 poster board
- ☐ 8' sheet of butcher paper
- ☐ clean socks (1 sock each for half the class)
- ☐ gumdrops
- ☐ toothpicks
- ☐ a heavy book
- ☐ *On the Fast Track! #2* take-home paper
- ☐ *StationMaster Card #2*
- ☐ *(optional)* treasure box
- ☐ *(optional)* snack: flour tortillas, cheese sticks
- ☐ *(optional)* Activity #2: index cards, markers or crayons, stapler

GET SET!

(Lesson Preparation)

- ■ Print today's Bible memory verse on a poster board: **And we have seen and testify that the Father has sent his Son to be the Savior of the world (1 John 4:14).**
- ■ Make a copy of *On the Fast Track! #2* take-home paper for each child.
- ■ Make a copy of *StationMaster Card #2* for each helper.
- ■ Set out the Celebration Calendar and *(optional)* treasure box.
- ■ Set up snack and outside play activities if you include these items in your children's ministry.

TICKETS PLEASE!

(Welcome and Bible Connection)

- ■ *Objective: To excite children's interest and connect their own life experiences with the Bible Truth, children will make a mural about families and talk about their experiences expecting new babies.*

When you see this icon, it means preparation will take more than five minutes.

Welcome Time Activity: Waiting for Baby Mural

■ *Materials: 8' sheet of butcher paper, markers or crayons*
Tape the sheet of paper to a blank wall at children's eye level with a tub of markers or crayons on the floor beside it. As kids arrive, direct them to make pictures of families with children, including babies. As they draw, ask them to share any experiences they've had when waiting for new babies to be born.

Sharing Time and Bible Connection

When everyone has arrived, call children to the lesson area and welcome them. Introduce the lesson by discussing the following questions. As you talk, give every child the opportunity to say something. Acknowledge the families and babies children drew during the Welcome Time Activity.

■ **What kinds of things do parents do when they know a new baby is coming?** (make a nursery, buy new clothes for the mother and baby, choose a name, etc.)

■ **Show me with your faces how people feel when they find out a new baby is coming to their family.** Observe and affirm children's expressions.

A lot of you smiled, but no one laughed. The Bible tells us about someone who did laugh when God said he and his wife would have a baby. This was amazing news! This baby was the beginning of a new family—and from this family would come the One God promised to save people from their sin.

ALL ABOARD FOR BIBLE TRUTH!   Genesis 17, 21
(Bible Discover and Learn Time)

■ *Objective: Children will study Genesis 17 and 21 to learn how God promised a Savior from the days of Abraham as God's solution to our sin.*

■ *Materials: gumdrops, toothpicks, a heavy book*

Last week our Bible story ended with a very big problem. Do you remember what it was? (Adam and Eve sinned, they broke their friendship with God)

Sin was a problem no person could solve. Only God could do that. But God had a plan—and it was a very good one. His plan began a long, long time ago with a *covenant.* **What's a covenant?** Let children respond. **A covenant is a promise between**

two people or groups of people. Each person contracts or agrees to do something, and both must keep his side of the agreement. **How about if you and I make a contract? I have this bag of gumdrops.** Show them. **I agree to share these gumdrops with you today. But you must agree to listen very well to the Bible story and answer some questions later. That's our contract. Do you all agree?** Allow children's response. **Of course, your contract is just with me about a few gumdrops.**

In Genesis 17, God made a contract or covenant with a man named Abraham. In Abraham's time, many people served false gods. But Abraham worshipped only the one true God. He agreed to serve God and no one else. That was Abraham's part of the covenant.

In return, God agreed to give Abraham and his wife Sarah a huge family. And from Abraham's family would come the Savior of the world. How Abraham laughed! How could he and Sarah have a huge family? Abraham was already 99 years old and they had no children.

Abraham laughed because he thought God's promise was impossible. **Why, that would be like saying these tiny toothpicks and gumdrops can hold the weight of this heavy book 5 inches above the table. Do you think they can?** Show children the gumdrops and toothpicks, then pass around the book for children to feel its weight. Ask a volunteer to try to stack up gumdrops and toothpicks on a table.

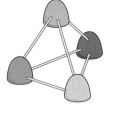
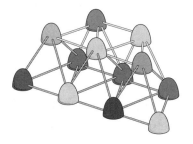

We can't get the stack high enough. It seems impossible.

What God said seemed impossible, too. But <u>God had promised a Savior</u> and he always keeps his promises. Nothing is impossible for God. Gather children around the table. Pass each child several toothpicks and gumdrops and give them a few minutes to try to build a support for the book. If no one is successful, demonstrate how to build a pyramid of toothpicks with a gumdrop at each joint. Connect several pyramids to form a sturdy structure. Place the textbook on top and see how it holds. **It wasn't impossible, was it? We understand how this experiment works because triangular structures are so strong, but God can do impossible things that no one can explain.**

Did God keep his part of the covenant? Yes! The next year, when Abraham was 100 years old, he and Sarah had a baby they named Isaac. Isaac grew up and had many children of his own. The family grew and grew until one day, generations later, <u>a Savior was born, just as God had promised.</u> God had a plan to free us from our sin and it began with a promise. God kept his promise.

Use the Clues!
(Bible Review)

Let's find out what you remember.

■ **What's a covenant?** (an agreement between two people, like a contract)
■ **Why did God make a covenant with Abraham?** (it was the start of his promise to send a Savior, Abraham's family was the beginning of the family line of the Savior)
■ **What did Abraham do when he heard God's plan?** (he laughed)
■ **How did God keep his part of the covenant?** (he gave Abraham and Sarah a baby even though they were already very old)
■ **What does this story teach us about God?** (God keeps his promises, he can do the impossible, God had a plan to take care of our sin)

If children kept their part of the covenant by listening well to the story, let them eat the gumdrops from their triangles if they desire, and distribute the rest evenly among the class. **You kept your part of the covenant, so I'm keeping mine.**

Show the children the Celebration Calendar and remind them that the symbol inside each door will help them remember what they learned from the Bible that week. Ask a volunteer to open door #1 and recall what the tree stands for (the first sin, the tree of the knowledge of good and evil). **What symbol do you think could stand for what we learned today from the Bible?** Let kids call out their ideas. Choose a volunteer to open door #2. **How does a baby remind us of today's story?** (God kept his promise to give Abraham and Sarah a baby, the baby was the start of God's promise to send a Savior)

BIBLE MEMORY WAYPOINT   1 John 4:14
(*Scripture Memory*)

■ *Objective: Children will hide God's Word in their hearts for guidance, protection, and encouragement.*
■ *Materials: clean socks*

And we have seen and testify that the Father has sent his Son to be the Savior of the world (1 John 4:14).

Read the verse from the poster. Then have the children read it with you as you point to the words. Give half the children (the stronger readers) a sock and show them how to make a sock puppet by slipping the sock over one hand. Pair up another child with each puppeteer. The puppeteer will teach the other child the verse, phrase by phrase. After a few minutes of practice, have the other child take the sock and repeat the verse to the partner using the puppet.

PRAYER STATION

- ■ *Objective: Children will explore and practice prayer for themselves in small groups.*
- ■ *Materials: copies of StationMaster Card #2 for each adult or teen helper*

Break into small groups of three to five children. Assign a teen or adult helper to each small group and give each helper a copy of *StationMaster Card #2* (see Resources) with ideas for group discussion and prayer.

SNACK STOP: BABIES IN A BLANKET (Optional)

If you plan to provide a snack, this is an ideal time to serve it.

- ■ *Materials: flour tortillas, cheese sticks*

Pass out a tortilla and a cheese stick to each student. Have them lay the cheese in the center and bundle up the tortilla around it like a baby being wrapped in a blanket. Talk about how different life would have been for Isaac compared to life for kids today (no toys, no TV or video games, living in a tent, walking long distances, etc.), and how Isaac was the beginning of God's promise to send a Savior.

Note: Always be aware of children with food allergies and have another option on hand if necessary.

APPLICATION

- ■ *Objective: Children will have opportunities to show how the lesson works in their own lives through activities and take-home papers.*

Some children's ministries may allow children to play outside at this point. If yours does not, choose one of the following activities.

Story True or False

Designate one wall or end of the playing area as the "true" side and the opposite end "false," and then gather children in the middle of the playing area. You'll read a statement about the Bible story and children will run to either the true or the false end, depending on what they believe about your statement. For false statements, ask children what would make it true. You can add more variety by having children move in other ways, such as crab walk, hop, shuffle, etc.

God made a covenant with Isaac. (false, it was with Abraham)

Abraham laughed when God said he and Sarah would have a baby. (true)

Abraham didn't think God could do the impossible. (true)

Abraham was very young when God made a covenant with him. (false, he was already old)

God's plan was for the Savior to come from Abraham's family. (true)

Sometimes God keeps his promises. (false, he keeps all his promises)

Covenant Capers

■ *Materials: index cards, markers or crayons, stapler*

Give each student five index cards. Have them write a promise to do something on each card (for example, "I promise to set the table two times this week"). Staple the edges of the cards together to make a booklet. This week, students can distribute their cards to family and friends as a promise to do something for them. Remind them that they need to fulfill their promises!

Tell students that each time they keep a promise, they can remember how God fulfilled his promise to Abraham and sent him a son.

ON THE FAST TRACK! *(Take-Home Papers)*

Collect tickets from children who completed last week's take-home work and let them choose something from the treasure box. **Remember, every time you take your *On the Fast Track!* paper home and do the activities, ask your parents to sign the ticket. You can bring the signed ticket back for a prize.**

Distribute the take-home papers and covenant booklets, if made, just before children leave.

LESSON THREE: Ruth Becomes Part of God's Promise

Memory Verse:

When Jesus spoke again to the people, he said, **"I am the light of the world. Whoever follows me will never walk in darkness,** but will have the light of life" (John 8:12).

Early elementary verse in **bold** *type.*

Bible Basis:
Book of Ruth

Bible Truth:
We can trust God to do what is best.

You Will Need:

- [ ] Celebration Calendar (with all doors closed again)
- [ ] 1 poster board
- [ ] assorted U.S. coins (pennies, nickels, dimes, and quarters)
- [ ] *(optional)* magnifying glasses
- [ ] 6 paper sacks
- [ ] baggie of dry dirt and small rocks
- [ ] facial tissue box
- [ ] dried grain
- [ ] small baby blanket
- [ ] sandal
- [ ] baby doll
- [ ] Bibles
- [ ] bookmarks
- [ ] *On the Fast Track! #3* take-home paper
- [ ] *StationMaster Card #3*
- [ ] *(optional)* treasure box
- [ ] *(optional)* snack: whole wheat crackers
- [ ] *(optional)* Activity #1: bag of foam packing peanuts, set of chopsticks for each team, paper lunch bags, box
- [ ] *(optional)* Activity #2: paper, pencils, markers, whiteboard, clear contact paper or laminating equipment, grain sheaf example

GET SET!
(Lesson Preparation)

- ■ ⏱ Print today's Bible memory verse on a poster board, but leave off key words. Instead, print just the first letter of the following words, with a line for the rest of the word: *Jesus, people, light, world, follows, walk, darkness, light, life.*

  When Jesus spoke again to the people, he said, "I am the light of the world. Whoever follows me will never walk in darkness, but will have the light of life" (John 8:12).

- ■ Place the baggie of dry dirt and small rocks, facial tissue box, dried grain, small baby blanket, sandal, and baby doll each in a paper sack. Number them 1–6 in order of the list (i.e. dirt is #1, facial tissue box is #2, etc.). Set the 6 sacks in the story area.

- ■ ⏱ Number four bookmarks 1–4, then print one of the following references on each one. Bookmark four Bibles at the correct passages and place them in the story area:
  1. Ruth 1:16–17
  2. Ruth 2:20
  3. Ruth 3:3–4
  4. Ruth 3:10–11.

- ■ If using Activity #2, make a copy of the grain sheaf example to show the children (see Resources).

- ■ Make a copy of *On the Fast Track! #3* take-home paper for each child.

- ■ Make a copy of *StationMaster Card #3* for each helper.

⏱ *When you see this icon, it means preparation will take more than five minutes.*

- Set out the Celebration Calendar and (optional) treasure box.
- Set up snack and outside play activities if you include these items in your children's ministry.

TICKETS PLEASE!
(Welcome and Bible Connection)

- **Objective:** *To excite children's interest and connect their own life experiences with the Bible Truth, children will compare different types of coins.*

Welcome Time Activity: Coin Examination

- **Materials:** *assorted U.S. coins—pennies, nickels, dimes, and quarters; magnifying glasses (optional)*

As children arrive, direct them to the table with the coins. Let children examine the coins and compare them. They can work with one or two partners or alone. Have them make a list (an older child or helper can write ideas) of how the coins are alike.

Sharing Time and Bible Connection

When everyone has arrived, call children to the lesson area and welcome them. If you didn't use the Welcome Time Activity, incorporate it in this introduction and then proceed to the questions below.

Begin today's lesson by discussing the following questions. As you talk, give every child the opportunity to say something.

- **What parts of all coins are the same**? (round, made of metal, dates, words)
- **What four words are on the front, or face side, of every coin?** (In God We Trust)
- **What does it mean to trust God?** (to believe that God will do what is best, to know that God will keep his promises)
- **God has a good plan for each of us. Sometimes, when things don't seem to be going well for us, that is hard to remember, isn't it? Did you have a time like that this week?** Let children share.

Even when things don't seem to be going well, God still has a plan. We can trust God to do what is best and that his plans are good ones. The Old Testament tells us about someone who trusted God, even though everything seemed to be going wrong for her. Let's dig in and discover how Ruth trusted God and became part of his plan to send a Savior.

ALL ABOARD FOR BIBLE TRUTH

Book of Ruth

(Bible Discover and Learn Time)

- ■ **Objective:** *Children will study the book of Ruth to realize that when Ruth trusted God to do what was best, she became part of God's plan to send the Savior.*
- ■ **Materials:** *numbered paper sacks holding dry dirt, facial tissue box, dried grain, small baby blanket, sandal, baby doll; bookmarked Bibles*

Hand out the six sacks to different children and distribute the four bookmarked Bibles to confident readers. When you reach the numbered parts of the story, the child with that number sack should pull out what's inside and show the class. When you come to a bookmarked passage, have the child with that bookmark read the corresponding verses.

Today's story is about a woman who had a part in God's plan to send a Savior to earth. She was from a country called Moab. Our story starts when Israel was having a famine. Sack #1. **That means that crops didn't grow that year, so there was no food. People were starving. One man named Elimelech, who lived in Bethlehem, took his family out of Israel to escape starvation. He and his wife Naomi and their two sons went to Moab. The sons soon married women in Moab. But later, Elimelech and both the sons died. That left Naomi with her daughters-in-law. They were all very sad.** Sack #2. **One of the wives was named Ruth. When Naomi decided to go back to Bethlehem, her hometown, she didn't expect Ruth or the other wife to go with her. They were from Moab, so why would they leave their own country?**

But Ruth had another idea. Listen to what she told Naomi. Bookmark #1, Ruth 1:16–17. **So they started the long walk back to Bethlehem. Naomi was so sad about losing her husband and sons. But Ruth didn't give up.** <u>She trusted in God to do what was best</u> **for her and Naomi.**

At that time, women couldn't work for money. The only way to get food in Bethlehem was to gather leftover grain in some farmer's field. So that's what Ruth did. She went out to a field and started picking up leftover bits of grain. Sack #3. **Ruth and Naomi kept from starving by eating that grain.**

It turned out that the owner of the field was a relative of Naomi's. Do you think that was an accident? No! God was doing the best thing for Ruth because she trusted him. The owner of the field, Boaz, admired Ruth's hard work.

When Naomi asked where Ruth was getting the grain, she was excited. Bookmark #2, Ruth 2:20. **God was taking care of them!**

Naomi gave Ruth advice. It sounds strange to us, but it was part of their custom. Bookmark #3, Ruth 3:3–4. **Ruth said she would do exactly as Naomi suggested.**

Stage whisper. **When Boaz was sleeping, Ruth snuck over and uncovered his feet.** Sack #4. **She laid down next to his feet. When he woke up, was Boaz ever surprised! "Who are you?" he asked. Ruth explained she was a relative. Do you think Boaz was mad?** Bookmark #4, Ruth 3:10–11. <u>**Ruth saw again how God was doing what was best.**</u>

Boaz had to make sure no one else wanted to marry Ruth. He followed another custom, and met the men of the city at the city gate. He offered the field that belonged to Naomi's dead husband to another relative to buy. That man didn't want it. So to show Boaz could buy it instead, the man took off his sandal and handed it to Boaz. Sack #5. Guess what? That field wasn't the only thing Boaz got. It also meant he had to marry Ruth, which is what he wanted to do!

When Boaz and Ruth got married, Naomi had a good place to live and enough food. And soon Ruth and Boaz had a baby. Sack #6. They named him Obed. This baby would grow up to be the grandfather of a very important king, who was also going to be part of the Savior's family. But that story is for next week.

Use the Clues!
(Bible Review)

Let's find out what you remember about today's story.

■ **What kind of a woman was Ruth?** (faithful, loving, hard working, a servant, humble)

■ **What did Ruth believe about God?** (he would do what was best when she trusted him)

■ **How was Ruth a part of God's plan to send a Savior?** (she trusted God and had a baby who would be part of the Savior's family)

■ **What can we expect when we trust God?** (He will do what is best for his kingdom)

What symbol do you think could stand for what we learned from the Bible today? Let kids call out ideas. Choose a volunteer to open door #3. **How does a stalk of grain remind us of today's story?** (Ruth met Boaz when she was picking up grain, and they had a baby who would be part of the Savior's family)

Choose a volunteer to open door #1 and tell what the tree stands for (the first sin). Repeat with door #2. (God's promise to send a Savior started with Abraham's baby, Isaac).

BIBLE MEMORY WAYPOINT   John 8:12
(Scripture Memory)

■ **Objective:** *Children will hide God's Word in their hearts for guidance, protection, and encouragement.*

■ **Materials:** *Bibles*

When Jesus spoke again to the people, he said, "I am the light of the world. Whoever follows me will never walk in darkness, but will have the light of life" (John 8:12).

Read the verse with its missing words from the poster board. Hand out Bibles to small groups of students and have them look up the reference. As a large group, have children raise their hands to name the missing words as you write them in the correct spaces. After each word is filled in, have the children read the verse aloud with you. Once all the words are written in on the poster, let volunteers recite the verse from memory.

PRAYER STATION

- ◼ **Objective:** *Children will explore and practice prayer for themselves in small groups.*
- ◼ **Materials:** *copies of* StationMaster Card #3 *for each adult or teen helper*

Break into small groups of three to five children. Assign a teen or adult helper to each small group and give each helper a copy of *StationMaster Card #3* (see Resources) with ideas for group discussion and prayer.

SNACK STOP: GLEANIN' GRAINS (Optional)

If you plan to provide a snack, this is an ideal time to serve it.

- ◼ **Materials:** *whole wheat crackers*

Pass around the crackers and ask children what they're made of (whole wheat). Explain that we don't eat a lot of barley these days, which is a grain Ruth gathered. Have children brainstorm other kinds of grains that they eat, such as corn, wheat, and rice, and talk about some things they might be used for.

Note: Always be aware of children with food allergies and have another option on hand if necessary.

APPLICATION

- ◼ **Objective:** *Children will have opportunities to show how the lesson works in their own lives through activities and take-home papers.*

Some children's ministries may allow children to play outside at this point. If yours does not, choose one of the following activities.

Gleaning Relay

■ *Materials: bag of foam packing peanuts, set of chopsticks for each team, paper lunch bags, box*

Remind the children what gleaning is: after workers have harvested the crop from a field, people who need food can pick up whatever is left over in the field. It wasn't easy! Kids will be gleaners in this game. Tape start lines and finish lines for this relay, then toss a pile of packing peanuts on the floor at each finish line. Put a large box at each start line. Line up the children in equal teams and give the first person in each line a pair of chopsticks and a lunch bag. Instruct kids to run to the pile of peanuts and use the chopsticks to put 10 of them into the bag, then run back to the start line and dump the peanuts into the box. Hand the chopsticks and bag to the next in line and repeat. First team to have everyone complete the task wins. After the game, have children discuss how God has done what's best for them, even if it's not always what they desire. Repeat the Bible Truth together: **We can trust God to do what is best.**

 ## Placemats

■ *Materials: paper, pencils, markers, whiteboard, clear contact paper or laminating equipment, grain sheaf example*

Write the Bible Truth, <u>**We can trust God to do what is best**</u>, on the board. Have children write or draw representative symbols or pictures of this Bible truth on a  sheet of paper and add decorative elements. If possible, have a sample drawing of a sheaf of grain (see illustration) available for the children to copy. Use contact paper or laminate each child's page to make a sturdy placemat. Challenge them to use this placemat at home this week as a reminder of the good things we trust God for each day.

 ## ON THE FAST TRACK! *(Take-Home Papers)*

If you brought your signed tickets today, come and choose something from the treasure box. Don't forget to do the *On the Fast Track!* activities this week and ask your parents to sign your ticket!

Distribute the take-home papers and placemats, if made, just before children leave.

LESSON FOUR: From Shepherd to King

Memory Verse:

The LORD does not look at the things man looks at. **Man looks at the outward appearance, but the LORD looks at the heart (1 Samuel 16:7).**

*Early elementary verse in **bold** type.*

Bible Basis:
1 Samuel 16—2 Samuel 7:16; Acts 13:23

Bible Truth:
The Savior comes from a royal family.

You Will Need:

- [ ] Celebration Calendar
- [ ] 1 poster board
- [ ] Bible time dress-up box
- [ ] additional dress-up items (crowns, royal robes, scepters, jewels, etc.)
- [ ] (optional) shepherd's staff
- [ ] On the Fast Track! #4 take-home paper
- [ ] StationMaster Card #4
- [ ] (optional) snack: small plain doughnuts or bagels, colored frosting in a squeeze container with decorator tip, raisins, and dried cranberries
- [ ] (optional) Activity #1: white or chalk board and markers or chalk, 2-liter bottles partially filled with water (3 per team), four plastic rings per team (can be made of coffee can lids with centers cut out to leave 1" rings), masking tape
- [ ] (optional) Activity #2: paper, scissors, markers or crayons, heart stickers or glitter glue or puff paint

When you see this icon, it means preparation will take more than five minutes.

GET SET!
(Lesson Preparation)

- ■ Print today's Bible memory verse on a poster board:
  The LORD does not look at the things man looks at. Man looks at the outward appearance, but the LORD looks at the heart (1 Samuel 16:7).
- ■ Make a copy of *On the Fast Track! #4* take-home paper for each child.
- ■ Make a copy of *StationMaster Card #4* for each helper.
- ■ Set out the Celebration Calendar and *(optional)* treasure box.
- ■ ⏱ *(Optional)* Activity: paint two of the 2-liter bottles purple (for royalty). These will be the center bottles for the ring toss game.
- ■ Set up snack and outside play activities if you include these items in your children's ministry.

TICKETS PLEASE!
(Welcome and Bible Connection)

- ■ **Objective:** *To excite children's interest and connect their own life experiences with the Bible Truth, children will pretend to be members of royalty.*

Welcome Time Activity: King and Queen for a Day

■ *Materials: Bible time dress-up box, extra dress-up items such as crowns, royal robes, jewels, scepters, etc.*

As children arrive, have them play a version of "Simon Says." One student will dress up as a king or queen and be "Simon" using the phrase: "King Says" or "Queen Says." Allow students to take turns as the king or queen as time permits.

Sharing Time and Bible Connection

When everyone has arrived, call children to the lesson area and welcome them. As you discuss these questions in preparation for the Bible story, give every child an opportunity to say something.

■ **What do you think it would be like to be a king or queen?**
■ **How does a person get chosen to be king or queen?** (they are born into a royal family, they are popular)
■ **What do you think are important qualities to be a good king or queen?** (kindness, wisdom, justice)

Not many of us have ever seen a real king or queen in person, but many countries today still have royal leaders. Back in Bible times, the Jewish people had kings. One king's family was part of God's plan for the Savior of the world to come! Let's find out how God chose that king.

 ALL ABOARD FOR BIBLE TRUTH 1 Samuel 16–2 Samuel 7:16; Acts 13:23
(Bible Discover and Learn Time)

■ *Objective: Children will study 1 and 2 Samuel and Acts 13:23 to find out that the Savior descended from David, a shepherd boy who became an important king.*
■ *Materials: Bible time dress-up box, crown (toy or paper), shepherd's staff (optional)*

Ask for eight volunteers, boys or girls. In small classes, children can take double roles. Ask one volunteer to stand off to the side and hold the shepherd's staff. The seven other volunteers should choose something from the dress-up box to help them act out the parts of David's brothers. Encourage these seven to show off their muscles, look strong and tough, and try to give their best impression. You will play the role of Samuel.

Today we're going to find out how God chose a new king for Israel. This king would have a very important job. But even more special is that he would be part of God's plan to send the Savior.

The Old Testament book of Samuel tells us that one of Israel's kings was named Saul. He was a good leader for a while, but then he stopped following God. So God told him that he could no longer be king. God had a better plan.

God sent a prophet named Samuel to choose a new king. "Find Jesse in Bethlehem," God told Samuel. "I'll show you who to choose as the new king." So Samuel walked to Bethlehem and found the man named Jesse.

Jesse had lots of sons. Eight, to be exact. Have your seven actors stand in a line in front of the class. **First, Samuel looked at Jesse's son Eliab.** Stand in front of the first actor who should show off his strength and look kingly. **"Surely the one God wants as king is standing right in front of me,"** Samuel thought.

Then God spoke to Samuel. **"Don't be impressed by what he looks like on the outside. This is not the one I've chosen." Oops! Samuel moved on to Jesse's next son, Abinadab.** As you mention each of the seven sons, move down the line of actors. Samuel waited to hear from God. No, this wasn't the one to be king.

Next Jesse sent his son Shammah to present himself to Samuel. "Was this the one?" Samuel wondered. "No," God told him. One by one, seven of Jesse's boys stood in front of Samuel. Each one was healthy and strong and good looking.

But after all seven had come and gone, God had not told Samuel to choose any of them. Samuel was puzzled and confused. What was going on here?

So he asked Jesse, "Do you have any other sons?"

"Yes," Jesse said. "I do have one more boy. He's the youngest and the smallest. He's out taking care of my sheep." Samuel wondered how God was going to make this work out. "Well, you'd better have him come in here," Samuel told Jesse.

What do you imagine Samuel was thinking as he waited for this young boy to come from the sheep pasture?

Have the David actor walk to the front of the room. **When the young man finally walked in, Samuel saw his red cheeks, beautiful eyes, and handsome appearance. But he knew God wasn't interested in how the young man looked. God wanted someone who had the right heart, who loved and honored him.**

"That's him!" God told Samuel. David was God's choice. Put the crown on "David." **God knew how to find a king. He looked at the person's heart, not how the person looked on the outside. David followed God from the inside out.**

David did become the king of Israel. But God's plan for him was even more important than that. God had a plan to send someone to free his people from their sin, and David became the great, great, great, great grandfather of the Savior. The Savior came from the royal family of David!

Use the Clues!
(Bible Review)

Let's review today's story.

■ **Why did God choose a new king for Israel?** (because King Saul stopped following God)

■ **How did Samuel know which of Jesse's sons was the one God wanted as king?** (God told him who to choose)

■ **What was important to God in this new king?** (a heart that loved God, what was inside)

■ **How was David part of God's plan to send a Savior?** (David was Jesus' great, great, great, great grandfather)

Here's our Celebration Calendar. **What symbol do you think is behind door #4 that will remind us about what we learned today from the Bible?** Let kids call out ideas. Choose someone to open door #4. **How does a crown remind us of today's story?** (it reminds us that David was made the king, it tells us that the Savior came from a royal family) Continue the review by letting different volunteers open the doors of previous weeks and tell about the symbols.

BIBLE MEMORY WAYPOINT   1 Samuel 16:7
(Scripture Memory)

■ ***Objective:*** *Children will hide God's Word in their hearts for guidance, protection, and encouragement.*

The LORD does not look at the things man looks at. Man looks at the outward appearance, but the LORD looks at the heart (1 Samuel 16:7).

Read the verse from the poster board. Then have the children read it with you as you point to each word. Make up actions for some of the words and phrases. Example: for "does not look at," wag a finger and shake your head 'no,' or have girls preen and boys flex biceps for "outward appearance." Ask a couple of children to join you in leading the verse practice. After rehearsing several times, let the class do the verse without your help.

PRAYER STATION

- ■ *Objective:* Children will explore and practice prayer for themselves in small groups.
- ■ *Materials:* copies of StationMaster Card #4 for each adult or teen helper

Break into small groups of three to five children. Assign a teen or adult helper to each small group and give each helper a copy of *StationMaster Card #4* (see Resources) with ideas for group discussion and prayer.

SNACK STOP: TASTEFUL CROWNS (Optional)

If you plan to provide a snack, this is an ideal time to serve it.

- ■ *Materials:* small plain doughnuts or bagels, colored frosting in a squeeze container with decorator tip, raisins, and dried cranberries

Let each child decorate a doughnut or bagel as a crown and add dried fruit pieces as jewels. Talk about the responsibilities that come with wearing a king or queen's crown: being a good example, making hard decisions, leading a country, following God's voice no matter what people say. Discuss how the Savior came from a royal family.

Note: Always be aware of children with food allergies and have another option on hand if necessary.

APPLICATION

- ■ *Objective:* Children will have opportunities to show how the lesson works in their own lives through activities and take-home papers.

Some children's ministries may allow children to play outside at this point. If yours does not, choose one of the following activities.

Draw-the-King Game

- **Materials:** *white or chalk board and markers or chalk, 2-liter bottles partially filled with water (3 per team), four rings per team, masking tape*

Teams will race to draw King David. Each team will draw their own king, composed of five segments: head and face, body, two arms, two legs, and crown. List these segments on the board for all to see; figures must be drawn in this order. To be able to draw each segment of their king, players must toss a ring around the center bottle in a line of 3 bottles.

Mark a line for each team to stand behind. At "go," the first player in each team will try to toss a ring over the center bottle in their group. Each player gets four tosses. If one makes the center bottle, that player runs to the board to draw the first king segment. Then the next player tosses. If all four of a player's tosses miss, he or she goes to the end of the line and the next player tries. Each team will need one or two players to retrieve rings and return them to the tossers. The first team to complete their King David drawing wins.

 ## Self-Portraits

- **Materials:** *paper, scissors, markers or crayons, heart stickers or glitter glue or puff paint*

Children will draw themselves, at least six inches tall, on a sheet of paper. The drawing should show them wearing their favorite clothes and best hair. After cutting out their self-portrait, have them draw a favorite coat, sweater or sweatshirt on the scrap paper. Show them how to add fold-back tabs to the sides of the shirt drawing and cut out the coat with the tabs. Demonstrate how to "put on" the coat by folding the tabs back over their portrait, like putting clothes on a paper doll. Then they'll remove the shirt and make a heart over their portraits' chest by applying a heart sticker or using glitter glue or puff paint. Ask them to show you how their portrait can be used to explain the memory verse.

 ## ON THE FAST TRACK! *(Take-Home Papers)*

Allow children who brought back signed tickets to choose something from the treasure box. **I'm excited to see how many people are bringing back their signed tickets! Keep up the good work.**

Hand out the take-home papers and self-portraits (if applicable) just before children leave.

LESSON FIVE: A Promise Is a Promise

The Prophets

Memory Verse:
I am the LORD, your God, the Holy One of Israel, your Savior (Isaiah 43:3).

Bible Basis:
Isaiah 7:14; 9:2, 6; 11:1–5; Micah 5:2

Bible Truth:
Prophets describe the Messiah—it's Jesus!

You Will Need:

- [ ] Celebration Calendar
- [ ] 1 poster board
- [ ] Bibles
- [ ] pushpins
- [ ] butcher paper
- [ ] overhead projector
- [ ] jar of treats
- [ ] *On the Fast Track! #5* take-home paper
- [ ] *StationMaster Card #5*
- [ ] *(optional)* treasure box
- [ ] *(optional)* snack: popcorn in a sack, juice or water
- [ ] *(optional)* Activity #1: copies of jigsaw puzzle page for each child, black markers, squares of various colored tissue paper, craft glue, shallow bowls or plastic lids (such as coffee can lids), unsharpened pencils

GET SET!
(Lesson Preparation)

- Print today's Bible memory verse on a poster board: **I am the LORD, your God, the Holy One of Israel, your Savior (Isaiah 43:3).**
- 🌐 Create the giant jigsaw puzzle for the Bible story by photocopying the jigsaw pattern (see Resources) onto a transparency, then projecting it on the wall. Tape butcher paper to the wall under the puzzle projection and use marker to create dotted lines where the pieces are cut apart. Use different colored markers to trace "Jesus." Cut apart the jigsaw pieces.
- Make a copy of *On the Fast Track! #5* take-home paper for each child.
- Make a copy of *StationMaster Card #5* for each helper.
- Print each of these references on a separate paper: Isaiah 7:14; Isaiah 9:2, 6; Isaiah 11:1–5; and Micah 5:2.
- Set out the Celebration Calendar and *(optional)* treasure box.
- *(Optional)* Activity: Make a copy of the jigsaw puzzle page for each child (see Resources). Cut various colors of tissue paper into 1 1/2" squares.
- Set up snack and outside play activities if you include these items in your children's ministry.
- Set out unassembled puzzles on tables for the Welcome Time Activity.

 When you see this icon, it means preparation will take more than five minutes.

TICKETS PLEASE!
(Welcome and Bible Connection)

■ **Objective:** *To excite children's interest and connect their own life experiences with the Bible Truth, children will assemble puzzles and describe what the puzzles create.*

Welcome Time Activity: Puzzle Play

■ **Materials:** *unassembled jigsaw puzzles*
As children arrive, direct them to the table of puzzles. They can work alone or with someone else (helper or child) to assemble a puzzle. As they begin, ask what they think the puzzle will be. When it's finished, ask those who worked it to describe what the puzzle shows.

Sharing Time and Bible Connection
When everyone has arrived, call children to the lesson area and welcome them.

■ **What is a promise?** (telling someone else that you'll do something)
■ **What kinds of promises has someone made to you?**
■ **What promises has God made to you and me?** (affirm answers)

I'm going to make you a promise right now: Before you leave today, I'm going to surprise you with something. But before that happens, we have some investigating to do.

ALL ABOARD FOR BIBLE TRUTH   Isaiah 7:14; 9:2, 6; 11:1-5; Micah 5:2
(Bible Discover and Learn Time)

■ **Objective:** *Children will study Isaiah and Micah to learn how the prophets described the Savior who would fulfill God's promise.*
■ **Materials:** *giant jigsaw puzzle pieces, pencils, Bibles, Bible references, tape, pushpins*

We know from the Old Testament that God promised to send a Savior—the Messiah—to free people from their sin. But who was he? What kind of Savior would he be? Let's see if we can find out.

Break the class into four mixed-age groups, with StationMasters assisting. Give each group one of the giant puzzle pieces and a paper with one of the Bible texts. (For large classes, cut the puzzle pieces in half using wavy cuts, and break down the Scripture portions to smaller amounts to spread around to a greater number of groups.)

Thousands of years ago, God told his prophets, Isaiah and Micah, about the Savior. What is a prophet? (a person who tells others what God says, someone who God talks to) **Each group has some words from Isaiah and Micah which describe the Messiah that God promised. We're going to read them and see what we find.**

Have each group look up their portion. A confident reader from each group should read it aloud as others follow along. Once groups have finished, each group should take a piece of the giant jigsaw puzzle and write or draw what their Bible text describes. They can write individual words or phrases, draw pictures to represent the words, or write the verse(s)—whatever they choose—to communicate the Scripture. Helpers can be sure children are representing the Scripture correctly, explain unclear meanings, and offer suggestions.

When all the groups are finished, have one or two members from each group bring their piece to the wall where you will assemble the puzzle. Use tape or tacks to hold the pieces in place on a wall or bulletin board as children fit them together. Allow group members to read what they wrote and tell what they drew.

The prophets Isaiah and Micah had lots to say about the Messiah God promised to send. With all these descriptions, and the way our puzzle looks, who were the prophets talking about? (Jesus) **Yes!** <u>**The prophets described the Messiah—it was Jesus**</u>**! Hundreds of years before Jesus was born as a human baby, God told the prophets what to tell his people. All these prophecies and promises came true with Jesus.**

Use the Clues!
(Bible Review)

Let's see what you remember.

■ **What is a prophet?** (a person who tells others God's words, someone who God talks to)

■ **What are some descriptions of the Messiah from Isaiah and Micah?** (any responses from the Scripture texts of the Bible story are acceptable)

■ **Our investigation led us to Jesus. He did come, just like the prophets had said. What does this tell us about God's**

promise? (God kept his promise, Jesus fulfilled God's promise)

What symbol do you think would remind us about what we learned today? Let kids call out ideas. Choose someone to open door #5. **How does a bright, shining candle remind us of today's story?** (it reminds us that Isaiah described Jesus as a great light that lights up the darkness)

Choose volunteers to open doors of previous weeks and tell what the symbols stand for. As you finish the review, remind the children that you made a promise to them and they are still waiting for you to fulfill the promise.

BIBLE MEMORY WAYPOINT
(Scripture Memory)

Isaiah 43:3

■ *Objective: Children will hide God's Word in their hearts for guidance, protection, and encouragement.*

I am the LORD, your God, the Holy One of Israel, your Savior (Isaiah 43:3).

Read the verse from the poster and then ask the children to read it with you slowly as you point to the words. To begin memorizing the verse, have the children get into groups of four and stand in a circle. One child will say "I am" and point to the next child who will state "the LORD your God." This child will then point to the next one who will add "the Holy One of Israel" and point to the last child who states "your Savior." In unison they will say the reference. Have them keep going, getting faster and more adept with the words until the verse is absorbed in their memories.

PRAYER STATION

■ *Objective: Children will explore and practice prayer for themselves in small groups.*
■ *Materials: copies of StationMaster Card #5 for each adult or teen helper*

Break into small groups of three to five children. Assign a teen or adult helper to each group and give each helper a copy of *StationMaster Card #5* (see Resources) with ideas for group discussion and prayer.

SNACK STOP: GUESSING GAME SNACK (Optional)

If you plan to provide a snack, this is an ideal time to serve it.

■ *Materials:* *popped popcorn hidden in a sack, juice or water*

I'm going to describe today's snack to you just like the prophets described Jesus, the Messiah. When you guess what it is, don't say anything. Just wait.

This snack is crunchy.

It makes noise when you make it.

Sometimes it's white, and sometimes it's yellow.

It starts out as a vegetable.

People like to put butter and salt on it.

When I count to "3" call out what you think I've been describing. After children have guessed, pass around the treat. While eating, children can play guessing games by describing something to each other to guess.

Have you thought about the promise I made to you earlier? Don't lose hope— I'll keep my promise soon.

Note: Always be aware of children with food allergies and have another option on hand if necessary.

APPLICATION

■ *Objective:* *Children will have opportunities to show how the lesson works in their own lives through activities and take-home papers.*

Some children's ministries may allow children to play outside at this point. If yours does not, choose one of the following activities.

The Promised One Collage

■ *Materials: copies of jigsaw puzzle page, black markers, squares of various colored tissue paper, craft glue, shallow bowls or plastic lids (such as coffee can lids), unsharpened pencils*

Children will make a colored collage of Jesus' name using the same template as you used for the Bible story puzzle. First have them outline *Jesus* with marker. Then show them how to take a tissue square, pinch it around the end of the pencil, and dip it into the glue. They will adhere the paper to *Jesus* inside the lines of the letters. When finished, the name *Jesus* will be a vibrant 3-D design.

 ## Free the Prisoners Tag

Play a version of freeze tag, but rename it "Free the Prisoners Tag" to help children remember that Jesus the Savior freed people from captivity to sin. Appoint two or more players as "It." They will run around trying to tag the others. Those tagged must freeze in place. They can be freed to play again if another player tags them and says "You are free!" After playing, ask children to imagine that people who haven't yet decided to ask Jesus to be their Savior are still frozen in their spirits by their sin. Jesus, the Savior and Messiah, frees them.

 ## ON THE FAST TRACK! *(Take-Home Papers)*

■ *Materials: jar of treats*

Before proceeding with this final element of the class, assemble the children and tell them that the promise you made to them will finally be fulfilled. **Who wondered if I would remember my promise? Did anyone think maybe I wouldn't do what I said?** As you let children choose a treat from your treat jar, help them understand that they had to wait for your promise just as God's people had to wait hundreds of years for God's promise of a Savior to come true. **Aren't you glad you didn't give up on my promise? Never give up on God's promises either.**

Allow the children with signed tickets to choose something from the treasure box, and remind them to complete the activities from *On the Fast Track!* and bring their signed tickets in.

If the children made a collage from Activity #1, distribute them along with the take-home papers before the children leave.

LESSON SIX: Jesus' Family Tree Has Long Roots

Family Tree

Memory Verse:
Wait for the LORD; be strong and take heart and wait for the LORD (Psalm 27:14).

Bible Basis:
Luke 3:23–38

Bible Truth:
People waited a long time for the Savior.

You Will Need:

- [ ] Celebration Calendar
- [ ] 1 poster board
- [ ] white or chalk board
- [ ] butcher paper
- [ ] *On the Fast Track! #6* take-home paper
- [ ] *StationMaster Card #6*
- [ ] *(optional)* treasure box
- [ ] *(optional)* snack: large clear jar of small snack pieces such as raisins, fish crackers, candy coated chocolate, pretzel sticks, etc.
- [ ] *(optional)* Activity #1: building blocks
- [ ] *(optional)* Activity #2: drawing paper, pencils, markers, Bibles

GET SET!
(Lesson Preparation)

- ■ Print today's Bible memory verse on a poster board: **Wait for the LORD; be strong and take heart and wait for the LORD (Psalm 27:14).**
- ■ On a 4–5" length of butcher paper *held vertically,* draw a family tree with a trunk and two main branches, left and right (see Resources).
- ■ Make a copy of *On the Fast Track! #6* take-home paper for each child.
- ■ Make a copy of *StationMaster Card #6* for each helper.
- ■ Set out the Celebration Calendar and *(optional)* treasure box.
- ■ Set up snack and outside play activities if you include these items in your children's ministry.
- ■ Set out markers or chalk at the board for the Welcome Time Activity.

TICKETS PLEASE!
(Welcome and Bible Connection)

- ■ *Objective: To excite children's interest and connect their own life experiences with the Bible Truth, children will express a situation where they had to wait.*

When you see this icon, it means preparation will take more than five minutes.

Welcome Time Activity: My Long Wait

■ *Materials:* *white or chalk board, whiteboard markers or chalk*
As children arrive, let them find a spot at the board and draw a picture showing a time they had to wait for something. Encourage them to think of a situation where they had to wait a long time.

Sharing Time and Bible Connection

When everyone has arrived, call children to the lesson area and welcome them. Ask children who drew pictures on the board during the Welcome Time Activity to show their picture and explain it. Comment on the various lengths of waiting time each picture represents.

■ **What other things have you waited for that seemed to take a long, long time?**
■ **How do you feel about waiting for something?** (impatient, tired, bored, frustrated)

We just don't like to have to wait for something we're looking forward to, do we? People back in Bible times felt the same way about waiting. In the Old Testament times, God had promised to send the Messiah and Savior, Jesus. But people had to wait a long, long time for that promise to be fulfilled. Do you want to guess how long? Give children a moment to guess. **Let's find out more about it!**

ALL ABOARD FOR BIBLE TRUTH   Luke 3:23-38
(Bible Discover and Learn Time)

■ *Objective: Children will study Luke 3:23–38 to learn about Jesus' earthly ancestors and how many generations it took before God's Savior came.*
■ *Materials: butcher paper family tree taped to the wall in the teaching area, markers*

Some of you guessed that people waited (lengths of time) **for the Messiah to come. We're going to find out about Jesus' family tree today. What is a family**

tree, anyway? (a picture that shows everyone in your family)

Direct kids' attention to the family tree. **If this were your family tree, your name would go here** (point to the trunk). **Above that would be a branch for your mom's name and a branch for your dad's name. Above your mom's name would be branches for her parents—your grandparents. Above your father's name would be branches for your other set of grandparents.** If children from stepparent homes or single family homes seem puzzled, assure them that there is a place on their family tree for every member of their family, even if they don't live with some of them. **Who do you think would be on the next level above your grandparents?** (their parents, or great grandparents) **Each level shows a lifetime, and it adds up to a long period of time, doesn't it?**

God was the father of Jesus. But Jesus had parents here on earth too. Did you ever think of Jesus having grandparents? Well, he did! Let's make a picture of Jesus' family tree.

Ask a child who's a confident writer to write Jesus' name on the tree trunk. Ask another to write Mary and Joseph on branches to the left and right above Jesus. **In Bible times, people only kept track of the names in the father's family, so we'll just have Joseph's family on Jesus' family tree.**

Ask children to line up in front of the tree. As you name each successive generation, a child will draw a simple branch above the previous one, starting right above Joseph and going up. The tree may look lopsided and odd, but will be a visual picture of the many generations between Adam and Jesus. You may wish to help some of the younger children.

I'll read the list of Jesus' ancestors, and you'll take turns drawing another branch up the tree. Read Luke 3:23–38, allowing children to cycle through the line as many times as needed to make a branch as you read each name. Read the names in this way: Jesus was the son of Joseph. Joseph was the son of Heli, etc.

Did any of the names I read sound familiar? (Jesse, David, Jacob, Joseph, Isaac, Abraham, Noah, Adam) **Some of these men lived hundreds of years. <u>They had to wait all their lives for the Savior</u>, and still didn't see him. This family tree shows that it was thousands of years from Adam to Jesus.**

How long have we had to wait? (not at all) **That's right, Jesus already came and died for us. We can have our sins forgiven by him as soon as we trust in him. We don't have to wait for our Savior like all these people did.**

Use the Clues!
(Bible Review)

Let's talk about what we learned today.

- **How long did some people wait for the Savior?** (all their lives, many years)
- **Who are some of the people who were in Jesus' family and who waited for him to come?** (Jesse, David, Isaac, Abraham, Noah, Adam, etc.)
- **Did God forget his promise to send a Savior?** (no, he kept his promise)

- **Are we still waiting today for a Savior to bring us forgiveness for our sins?** (no, Jesus already came)

What symbol do you think could stand for what we learned today from the Bible? Let kids call out ideas. Choose someone to open door #6. **How does a grandfather's face remind us of today's story?** (we're reminded that people had to wait many years for Jesus to come)

Choose volunteers to open doors of previous weeks and tell what the symbols stand for.

BIBLE MEMORY WAYPOINT   PSALM 27:14
(Scripture Memory)

- ***Objective:*** *Children will hide God's Word in their hearts for guidance, protection, and encouragement.*

Wait for the LORD; be strong and take heart and wait for the LORD (Psalm 27:14).

Read today's verse, pointing to each word as you read it. Then, form a circle while standing. Start the verse practice by saying the first word of the memory verse. The person to your right says the second word. The next person in line says the third word, etc. If a student says the wrong word or doesn't know the word, she can read the poster or get help from someone else. Try it a second time with everyone saying two words at a time or with the verse covered up.

PRAYER STATION

- **Objective:** *Children will explore and practice prayer for themselves in small groups.*
- **Materials:** *copies of* StationMaster Card #6 *for each adult or teen helper*

Break into small groups of three to five children. Assign a teen or adult helper to each small group and give each helper a copy of *StationMaster Card #6* (see Resources) with ideas for group discussion and prayer.

SNACK STOP: GUESS THE WAIT (Optional)

If you plan to provide a snack, this is an ideal time to serve it.

- **Materials:** *large clear jar of small snack pieces such as raisins, oyster or fish crackers, candy coated chocolate, pretzel sticks, etc.*

How many treats do you think are in this jar? If possible, give each child a chance to guess. **Think about how many years some people from Bible times had to wait for Jesus. Wow! We can enjoy all the blessings and goodness of salvation right now, and not have to wait like many people did.** Pass out some of the snack from the jar.

To add more excitement, count the number of snack pieces in the jar and determine which child came the closest with his or her guess.

Note: Always be aware of children with food allergies and have another option on hand if necessary.

APPLICATION

- **Objective:** *Children will have opportunities to show how the lesson works in their own lives through activities and take-home papers.*

Some children's ministries may allow children to play outside at this point. If yours does not, choose one of the following activities.

Family Towers

■ *Materials: building blocks*

Create groups of no more than eight children, depending on your class size and how many blocks you have. Each group will attempt to build a tower with lots of blocks to show the many generations of people in Jesus' family. (There were 76 generations before him.) You can make this a competitive team activity, racing to make the highest tower, or a cooperative activity with the groups endeavoring to achieve 76 blocks before the tower collapses. Suggest that more than one block be used for the foundation.

 Jesus' Family Tree

■ *Materials: drawing paper, pencils, markers, Bibles*

Children will draw an outline of a tree with a huge canopy (area where the branches and leaves are). In the canopy, have them draw pictures of any of Jesus' ancestors they can think of. For example, Noah could be pictured with an ark or a rainbow. David could be a shepherd with a staff. Abraham could sit on a camel or be in front of a tent. Have the Luke 3 genealogy available for those who want to read the list again.

 ON THE FAST TRACK! *(Take-Home Papers)*

Don't forget: complete the take-home activities from *On the Fast Track!* and bring in your signed tickets next week! Then you'll get to choose a fun prize from the treasure box.

Hand out the *On the Fast Track!* take-home papers before children leave.

LESSON SEVEN: The Big Announcement

Mary

Memory Verse:
This is love: not that we loved God, but that he loved us and sent his Son as an atoning sacrifice for our sins (1 John 4:10).

*Early elementary verse in **bold** type.*

Bible Basis:
Matthew 1:18–23;
Luke 1:26–38

Bible Truth:
God announces
his Son is coming.

You Will Need:

☐ Celebration Calendar
☐ white or chalk board
☐ white chenille stems
☐ Bible time dress-up box
☐ red construction paper
☐ *On the Fast Track! #7* paper
☐ *StationMaster Card #7*
☐ *(optional)* treasure box
☐ *(optional)* snack: angel cake or pound cake, angel cookie cutters, frosting, candy sprinkles, plastic knives
☐ *(optional)* Activity #1:
   inflated balloons with story segments
☐ *(optional)* Activity #2:
   copies of angel puppet template (see Resources), scissors, craft sticks, markers or gel pens, sequins, glue, foil, other art supplies as available

When you see this icon, it means preparation will take more than five minutes.

 GET SET!
(Lesson Preparation)

■ Print today's Bible memory verse on a whiteboard or chalkboard. Cut out three hearts out of red construction paper, big enough to cover the words "love" and "loved" on the board.
This is love: not that we loved God, but that he loved us and sent his Son as an atoning sacrifice for our sins (1 John 4:10).

■ Make two photocopies of the Bible story in this lesson. On one, highlight the part of Narrator 1. On the other copy, highlight the part of Narrator 2.

■ *(Optional)* Activity #1: Inflate eight balloons per team; depending on size of your class, you may have one or more teams. Each team will need a complete set of balloons. Write these brief phrases in permanent marker, one statement per balloon: Mary will have a son. Name the baby Jesus. He will be a king. His kingdom will not end. He'll save people from their sins. The baby is from the Holy Spirit. He is the Son of the Most High. Nothing is impossible with God.

■ Make a copy of *On the Fast Track! #7* take-home paper for each child.

■ Make a copy of *StationMaster Card #7* for each helper.

■ Set out the Celebration Calendar and *(optional)* treasure box.

■ Set up snack and outside play activities if you include these items in your children's ministry.

 # TICKETS PLEASE!
(Welcome and Bible Connection)

■ **Objective:** *To excite children's interest and connect their own life experiences with the Bible Truth, children will make angels from chenille stems.*

Welcome Time Activity: Angel Makers

■ **Materials:** *white chenille stems*

Have helpers create some examples of angels made from chenille stems. As children arrive, they can make their own angel, with a helper's assistance as needed. Be sure at least one of the angels is in plain view from where you will gather the children for the Bible story.

Sharing Time and Bible Connection

When everyone has arrived, call children to the lesson area and welcome them. As you talk, give every child the opportunity to say something.

Let's play a game of "I Spy." I'll give you clues and you try to guess what I'm talking about. The thing I'm thinking of is in this room, so look around as you think about my clues. Raise your hand to guess what it is. As you play this game, describe one of the angels a student created in the Welcome Time Activity.

    It's white (or whatever color the angel is).
    It's smaller than my Bible.
    It can't move by itself.
    It's fuzzy.
    Someone in the class made it.

Once someone guesses the angel, discuss what they know about angels.

■ **What do you think angels are like in real life?**
■ **Where have you heard about angels?** (Bible stories; children may have other sources)
■ **What is the job of an angel?** (to give a message from God to a person, to watch over people)

Angels are God's messengers. Today we're going to see how angels gave two people messages that really surprised them about the Messiah, the Savior everyone had been waiting for.

ALL ABOARD FOR BIBLE TRUTH

Matthew 1:18-23; Luke 1:26-38

(Bible Discover and Learn Time)

■ **Objective:** *Children will study Matthew 1 and Luke 1 to learn how angels heralded Jesus' coming.*

■ **Materials:** *Bible time dress-up box; two story scripts, each highlighted for a separate reader*

Ask for a boy volunteer and a girl volunteer to dress as Joseph and Mary. Ask for two other volunteers to dress as angels and give them appropriate props. Also choose two good readers. Each will read a portion from one of the Scripture texts.

As you hear the Bible story today, these actors and narrators are going to help you see it. Position Joseph a couple of feet to one side of you and Mary a couple of feet on the other side. The two angels should be behind where the class is seated, but in your view. Have the two narrators stand on either side of Mary and Joseph.

Today's story is about a very big announcement. Actually, it was two announcements, but the message was the same. After thousands of years of waiting for God's promised Messiah, our Savior, the time had finally come. So how do you think God let people know the Savior was about to show up? (he sent angels)

God sent one angel, named Gabriel, to a town called Nazareth. Motion to one angel to come stand near Mary. **The angel came to visit a young lady named Mary. She wasn't married yet, but she was engaged to Joseph. The angel talked to Mary.** (Narrator 1: "Greetings, favored one. The Lord is with you.")

What do you think Mary did when an angel just showed up and talked to her? Let children respond. **Yes, she was really surprised and wasn't sure what this greeting meant.** (Narrator 1: "Don't be afraid, Mary. God is pleased with you. You're going to have a baby son. Name him Jesus. He'll be the son of the Most High God. He will be a king and reign forever!")

Mary wondered how this would happen. She told the angel she wasn't married yet. (Narrator 1: "The Holy Spirit is going to cause you to have this baby. He will be called the Son of God.")

That wasn't the end of the surprises Mary had. The angel also said that her cousin Elizabeth (who was already old) was going to have a baby too! (Narrator 1: "Nothing is impossible with God.")

That was amazing! But Mary wasn't the only one who had an angel visit. Motion the other angel to come near to Joseph. **Joseph found out that Mary was going to have a baby. But they weren't married yet. That was a big problem! Maybe he shouldn't marry her after all. But one night, while he was sound asleep, an angel appeared to him too, in a dream.** (Narrator 2: "Joseph, son of David, don't be afraid to marry Mary. Her baby is from God. The baby will be a boy. You should name him Jesus because he's going to save people from their sins.")

Angels were the way <u>God announced that his son, the Savior, was coming</u>. The time would be soon. The long wait was nearly over.

Use the Clues!
(Bible Review)

I'm going to ask you a few questions about what we learned today.

- **What was the job of the angels in the story?** (they were messengers)
- **What did the first angel tell Mary?** (Mary would have a son, she should name him Jesus, he would be God's son and would reign forever)
- **Why was this good news?** (people had waited for a Messiah to free them from their sin for a very long time; the wait was nearly over)
- **What announcement did the other angel give to Joseph?** (Joseph should still marry Mary, her baby was from God, he should name him Jesus)

What symbol do you think could stand for what we learned today from the Bible? Let kids call out ideas. Choose someone to open door #7. **How does an angel remind us of today's story?** (it makes us think about the angels who announced that Jesus was coming)

Choose a volunteer to open doors of previous weeks and tell what the symbols stand for.

BIBLE MEMORY WAYPOINT   1 John 4:10
(Scripture Memory)

- *Objective: Children will hide God's Word in their hearts for guidance, protection, and encouragement.*
- *Materials: red hearts, tape, eraser, white or chalk board*

This is love: not that we loved God, but that he loved us and sent his Son as an atoning sacrifice for our sins (1 John 4:10).

Read the verse from the board. Then invite the children to read it with you as you point to the words. Put a tape loop on one heart and ask a child to place it over one of the "love" words. Repeat the verse together. Have two other children place the second and third heart on the other "love" words and say the verse in unison. Next, erase key words such as "sacrifice," "Son," "God," and "sins," saying the verse together after each erasure. Keep erasing words until children are very familiar with the verse.

PRAYER STATION

- **Objective:** *Children will explore and practice prayer for themselves in small groups.*
- **Materials:** *copies of* StationMaster Card #7 *for each adult or teen helper*

Break into groups of three to five children. Assign a teen or adult helper to each small group and give each helper a copy of *StationMaster Card #7* (see Resources) with ideas for group discussion and prayer.

SNACK STOP: ANGELIC TREATS (Optional)

If you plan to provide a snack, this is an ideal time to serve it.

- **Materials:** *thin slices of angel cake or pound cake, angel-shaped cookie cutters, plastic knives, frosting, candy sprinkles*

Let children share the cookie cutters to cut an angel from their cake. If you have no cookie cutters, show them how to cut an angel shape with a plastic knife. Let children spread frosting on the angels and top with sprinkles. As they eat their snack, ask them about announcements they've had that have been surprising (a new baby expected, a move, a visit from a relative, etc.)

Note: Always be aware of children with food allergies and have another option on hand if necessary.

APPLICATION

- **Objective:** *Children will have opportunities to show how the lesson works in their own lives through activities and take-home papers.*

Some children's ministries may allow children to play outside at this point. If yours does not, choose one of the following activities.

Pass the Message

■ **Materials:** *inflated balloons with story segments*

If you have a small class, play this game cooperatively as a single group. If you have a large class, divide into teams. Each team will need their own collection of balloons with the angels' announcements on them. Before starting, ask children to read the balloon message segments. Have children line up at one end of the room. Each team should choose one child to be Mary or Joseph and stand at the opposite end of the room. One by one, team members will take turns batting one balloon at a time across the room to their Mary or Joseph. The first team to have all their balloons reach their Mary or Joseph wins.

Angel Stick Puppets

■ **Materials:** *copies of angel puppet template (see Resources), scissors, craft sticks, markers or gel pens, sequins, glue, foil, other art supplies as available*

Direct children to cut out and decorate the angel using markers, gel pens, glitter glue, or foil pieces for clothing or halos. Use white glue to attach a craft stick to the back of the puppet. Give children time to practice retelling the story of the angels' announcements of the coming Savior.

ON THE FAST TRACK! *(Take-Home Papers)*

Can someone tell me how to get a prize from the treasure box? Allow children to respond. **That's right! When you take your** *On the Fast Track!* **paper home and do the activities, ask your parents to sign the ticket to show that you finished the work.**

Allow kids with tickets to collect their prizes from the treasure box, then distribute the take-home papers and stick puppets (if made) just before children leave.

LESSON EIGHT: Prepare the Way!

John the Baptist

Memory Verse:

Test me, O LORD, and try me, **examine my heart and my mind; for your love is ever before me,** and I walk continually in your truth (Psalm 26:2–3).

*Early elementary verse in **bold** type.*

Bible Basis:

Malachi 3:1–4

Bible Truth:

John the Baptist prepares the way for Jesus.

You Will Need:

- [ ] Celebration Calendar
- [ ] 1 poster board
- [ ] cloths
- [ ] brooms
- [ ] cleaning supplies
- [ ] Bible time dress-up box
- [ ] pretend microphone
- [ ] hat with press card
- [ ] towel
- [ ] trumpet or other horn
- [ ] felt tip pens
- [ ] *On the Fast Track! #8* take-home paper
- [ ] *StationMaster Card #8*
- [ ] *(optional)* treasure box
- [ ] *(optional)* snack: gummy worms, honey graham crackers or graham sticks, a squeeze bottle of honey
- [ ] *(optional)* Activity #1: paper, clear tape, markers or crayons, scissors
- [ ] *(optional)* Activity #2: masking tape

When you see this icon, it means preparation will take more than five minutes.

GET SET!
(Lesson Preparation)

- Print today's Bible memory verse on a poster board: **Test me, O LORD, and try me, examine my heart and my mind; for your love is ever before me, and I walk continually in your truth (Psalm 26:2–3).**
- Make a copy of *On the Fast Track! #8* take-home paper for each child.
- Make a copy of *StationMaster Card #8* for each helper.
- Set out the Celebration Calendar and *(optional)* treasure box.
- Set up snack and outside play activities if you include these items in your children's ministry.
- If you know someone who plays the trumpet or another horn, invite him or her to play a rousing fanfare at the beginning of your Sharing Time.

TICKETS PLEASE!
(Welcome and Bible Connection)

- **Objective:** *To excite children's interest and connect their own life experiences with the Bible Truth, children will clean the Sunday School classroom to prepare the way for the Savior.*

Welcome Time Activity: Preparing for Company

■ *Materials: cloths, brooms, cleaning supplies*
As children arrive, hand them cleaning supplies and tell them that you're preparing for a very special guest. Instruct them to dust, sweep, pick up, and sweep the room. It's an important guest and the room needs to be ready when he arrives.

Sharing Time and Bible Connection
■ *Materials: trumpet or other horn*

When everyone has arrived, call children to the lesson area and welcome them. As you lead into the discussion before the Bible story, give every child a chance to say something.

Have your guest trumpet player play a fanfare now, or if you have borrowed a horn, stand up and pretend to make the sound of a herald announcing an important person.

■ **Do you know what I was doing?** (playing a trumpet, making an announcement) **When a king or queen or other important person comes, there is an announcement so people can get ready.**
■ **What does your family do to get ready when they find out someone important is coming for a visit?** (clean up the house, make special food, dress in good clothes)

When God was ready to announce his son Jesus to the whole world, he sent messengers. What messengers did we talk about last week? (angels) **Today, we're going to find out about another unusual messenger God sent to tell the world to get ready for the Savior.**

📖 ALL ABOARD FOR BIBLE TRUTH   Malachi 3:1-4
(Bible Discover and Learn Time)

■ *Objective: Children will study Malachi 3 to learn how God used John the Baptist to prepare the way for the Savior.*
■ *Materials: Bible time dress-up box, pretend microphone, hat with press card, towel*

Today's lesson will simulate a TV newscast. Before the lesson, ask a male helper to read the role of John the Baptist while you play the part of the TV interviewer. Have the helper dress as John might have looked: unkempt hair, beard, a rough Bible-time cloak, bare feet, belt at the waist. Make an extra copy of this interview for "John" to read.

You might wear a hat with a press card in the brim. Hold a pretend microphone.

(John the Baptist is drying himself with a towel. Reporter approaches John and speaks into the microphone.)

Reporter: **This is** (name), **your on-the-spot reporter for Promise Radio. I am reporting from the edge of the Jordan River where there has been a lot of excitement lately. Let's talk with this man. Good morning, sir.**

John the Baptist: **Good morning.**

Reporter: **So, tell us who you are. Are you the Christ?**

John: **No, I'm not.**

Reporter: **No? Some people are saying that you are Elijah, the prophet. You do look kind of like him.**

John: **No, I am not Elijah either.**

Reporter: **Then, who are you?**

John: **My name is John the Baptist.** (With drama) **I am the voice calling in the desert, prepare the way for the Lord.**

Reporter: **Um, right. John, you look a mess. Your clothes are scruffy, your hair needs combing, and you've got no sandals on. Where have you been, man?**

John: **I've been living in the desert. It's not easy to take a bath there you know.**

Reporter: **I've heard that.**

John: **And searching for locusts and honey for supper is pretty hard on your sandals.**

Reporter: **You eat honey and locusts? Locusts are insects!**

John: **They're not bad—kind of crunchy. Want to try some** (reaching into pocket)**?**

Reporter: **I don't think so, but thanks for asking. So what brings you here to the Jordan River?**

John: **God gave me a message to tell people. He said, "Tell the people to get ready for Jesus."**

Reporter: **Who is Jesus?**

John: **Jesus is God's Son. He is the Messiah, the Savior who we have been waiting for these many years. The waiting hasn't been easy you know.**

Reporter: **What else did God tell you?**

John: **God wants people to get their hearts ready. He wants them to turn away from their sin and be baptized. I've been baptizing people here at this river for days.**

Reporter: **You must be very pleased by this.**

John: **Actually, it pleases God. When people turn away from sin and start obeying God with their words and actions, it pleases him.**

Reporter: **Did you say sin? I'm a pretty good guy. I mean, I don't break the law or anything ... well, except for the speed limit. But that's only when I'm really in a hurry. Ha, ha ...** (rueful grin).

John: **Every one of us has done wrong things that we need to get cleaned up. We can't do it ourselves, so God sent Jesus. <u>We need to prepare our hearts for him</u>. Well, I've got to get back to work now.**

Reporter: **Nice to meet you, John. Thanks for talking with me.**

John: (Walking "offstage") **Prepare the way for the Lord. Prepare the way for the Lord.**

Reporter: **You heard it here, folks. That was John the Baptist telling people to prepare for the coming of the Savior, the Messiah. This is** (name) **for Promise Radio. Thank you, and have a good day.**

Use the Clues!
(Bible Review)

Let's review a little bit about the lesson.
- **What was John the Baptist's job?** (<u>he prepared the way for Jesus</u>)
- **What message did John have for people?** (get ready for Jesus, the Savior)
- **What needs cleaning up in our own lives?** (our sin, the wrongs we've done)
- **How do we get our sin cleaned up?**

(admitting that we've done wrong and asking Jesus to clean up our sin)

What symbol do you think could stand for what we learned today from the Bible? Let kids call out ideas. Choose someone to open door #8. **How does a horn remind us of today's story?** (it's often used to announce something important to lots of people, and that's what John did)

Choose volunteers to open doors of previous weeks and tell what the symbols stand for.

BIBLE MEMORY WAYPOINT
(Scripture Memory)

Psalm 26:2-3

- ■ *Objective:* Children will hide God's Word in their hearts for guidance, protection, and encouragement.
- ■ *Materials:* felt tip pens

Test me, O LORD, and try me, examine my heart and my mind; for your love is ever before me, and I walk continually in your truth (Psalm 26:2–3).

Read this week's memory verse from the poster, pointing to each word. To help children memorize the verse, play "Finger Faces." Use a felt tip pen to draw eyes and a mouth on one index finger of each child. The children can make their finger face "talk" as they wiggle it. Divide the children into pairs, an older with a younger child, and let them make their finger faces say the verse to one another. You could also have the children walk around the room and make their finger faces repeat the verse to whomever they see. Encourage accuracy in saying the verse, even as they are having fun.

PRAYER STATION

- ■ *Objective:* Children will explore and practice prayer for themselves in small groups.
- ■ *Materials:* copies of StationMaster Card #8 for each adult or teen helper

Break into small groups of three to five children. Assign a teen or adult helper to each small group and give each helper a copy of *StationMaster Card #8* (see Resources) with ideas for group discussion and prayer.

SNACK STOP: LOCUSTS AND HONEY (Optional)

If you plan to provide a snack, this is an ideal time to serve it.

- ■ *Materials:* gummy worms, honey graham crackers or graham sticks, a squeeze bottle of honey

John the Baptist lived a very different life from other people in his time. He lived out in the wilderness and ate locusts, which are bugs, and honey. Let's pretend your gummy worms are locusts. Squeeze a small amount of honey on each child's graham cracker. If you'd like, talk about other foods that were more typical in John and Jesus' time: olives, dates, grapes and raisins, yogurt, onions, meat, pomegranates.

Note: Always be aware of children with food allergies and have another option on hand if necessary.

APPLICATION

■ **Objective:** *Children will have opportunities to show how the lesson works in their own lives through activities and take-home papers.*

Some children's ministries may allow children to play outside at this point. If yours does not, choose one of the following activities.

Messenger's Megaphone

■ **Materials:** *paper, clear tape, markers or crayons, scissors*

Children will make a megaphone to announce that Jesus is coming. First give them time to color and decorate their megaphone. Then roll it into a funnel shape and tape it to hold the shape. If desired, children can cut the wide end to make it evenly round. Allow them to use their megaphone to announce Jesus coming. If time permits, ask them questions from the Bible story and let them answer using their megaphones.

Prepare the Way! Game

■ **Materials:** *masking tape*

John the Baptist wanted to get people onto the path of following God. Make a masking tape line down the center of your play area. Line the children up facing a leader on the right side of the line. The right side of the line is "On the Path" and the left side of the line is "Off the Path." When the leader calls out either "On the Path" or "Off the Path," children must jump to the correct side of the line. If the children jump in the wrong direction they are out of the game. The last player left wins the game. The leader will try to make it hard by pointing to one side as they call out to jump to the other side, by repeating the same side, or by calling slower or faster.

ON THE FAST TRACK! *(Take-Home Papers)*

Collect any signed tickets and allow children to choose their prize from the treasure box. **Don't forget to ask your parents to sign your tickets whenever you do your *On the Fast Track!* activities. When you bring them in next week, you can choose a prize from the treasure box.**

Distribute *On the Fast Track! #8* before children leave.

LESSON NINE: Bethlehem Bound

Memory Verse:
The LORD himself goes before you and will be with you; he will never leave you nor forsake you. Do not be afraid; do not be discouraged (Deuteronomy 31:8).

*Early elementary verse in **bold** type.*

Bible Basis:
Micah 5:2;
Luke 2:1–5

Bible Truth:
God chose Bethlehem to be Jesus' birthplace.

You Will Need:

- [ ] Celebration Calendar
- [ ] 1 poster board
- [ ] butcher paper
- [ ] whiteboard
- [ ] Bible time map *(optional)*
- [ ] magazines
- [ ] Christmas CD/tape
- [ ] CD/tape player
- [ ] ball or unbreakable Christmas ornament
- [ ] *On the Fast Track! #9* take-home paper
- [ ] *StationMaster Card #9*
- [ ] *(optional)* treasure box
- [ ] *(optional)* snack: your choice of trail mix, dried fruit, cheese sticks, cheese crackers, or popcorn
- [ ] *(optional)* Activity #1: brown construction paper, pencils, scissors
- [ ] *(optional)* Activity #2: (per team) suitcase or duffel bag, towel, face cloth, pj's, shoes or slippers, hairbrush, toothpaste

 When you see this icon, it means preparation will take more than five minutes.

GET SET!
(Lesson Preparation)

- ▪ Print today's Bible memory verse on the poster board: **The LORD himself goes before you and will be with you; he will never leave you nor forsake you. Do not be afraid; do not be discouraged (Deuteronomy 31:8).**
- ▪ Bookmark your Bible at Micah 5:2.
- ▪ Make a copy of *On the Fast Track! #9* take-home paper for each child.
- ▪ Make a copy of *StationMaster Card #9* for each helper.
- ▪ Set out the Celebration Calendar and *(optional)* treasure box.
- ▪ Set up snack and outside play activities if you include these items in your children's ministry.

TICKETS PLEASE!
(Welcome and Bible Connection)

- ▪ **Objective:** *To excite children's interest and connect their own life experiences with the Bible Truth, children will share travel experiences and make a mural about packing for a trip.*

Welcome Time Activity: Get Packing Mural

■ *Materials: butcher paper, magazines, scissors, glue sticks*
Tape a 5–6' length of butcher paper to the wall at children's eye level and draw the outline of a suitcase on it. Set glue sticks, scissors, and magazines on the floor below the suitcase. As children arrive, ask them to search magazines for pictures of things they would pack to take on a trip. Have them cut out the pictures and glue them inside the suitcase drawing. As they work, ask them to tell about trips they've been on: Where did they go? How did they travel? Why did they go?

Sharing Time and Bible Connection

■ *Materials: whiteboard*

When everyone has arrived, call children to the lesson area and welcome them. Introduce today's lesson with the following activity.

You have told me about some wonderful trips that you've taken. Lots of you went to visit family and friends. Many of you went on vacation. But none of you went on a journey because of a census. What is a census? (a count of everyone who lives in a certain place) **Let's take a census of our class.** Choose one child as "census taker." **(Name of child) will be the census taker who will count our group.**

Call out categories such as boys, girls, children who are 7 years old, children who have a sister, those in blue clothing, etc. Those who belong to that group should stand while the census taker counts them and writes the number on the whiteboard.

In Bible times, rulers would take a census of all the people in their country. They wanted to know how many people should be paying taxes to them. That happened just before Jesus was born. Let's find out how it was part of God's plan.

ALL ABOARD FOR BIBLE TRUTH   Micah 5:2; Luke 2:1–5
(Bible Discover and Learn Time)

■ *Objective: Children will study Micah 5:2 and Luke 2:1–5 to learn how prophecy was fulfilled when Jesus was born in Bethlehem.*
■ *Materials: Bible bookmarked at Micah 5:2, Bible time map (optional)*

Who can tell me where you were born? Let children tell their birthplaces if they know them. **Hundreds of years before Jesus was born, God told his prophet Micah the**

name of the little town where the Savior would be born. **Remind me: who was the Savior?** (Jesus) **Listen while (name of child) reads the words from Micah and raise your hand if you hear the name of the town.** Ask a good reader to read Micah 5:2. Let children respond.

Yes, God said Jesus would be born in Bethlehem. But Mary and Joseph, Jesus' earthly parents, didn't live in Bethlehem. They lived in a town called Nazareth—that was 70 miles away! If you have a map, have a child locate both towns. **Would Mary's baby be born in Nazareth? Was God's word to Micah wrong? Of course not!** <u>God chose where Jesus would be born</u>. **It was part of his plan. And his plan even included Caesar Augustus—the most powerful ruler in the world.**

Not long before Jesus was going to be born, Caesar Augustus decided to count all the people under his rule so he could collect tax money from them. He told people they must travel to their hometowns to be counted. What was this counting called? (a census)

Joseph had to travel to his hometown and be counted too. Joseph had a relative a long time ago named David, the same one who was king. King David lived in Bethlehem. That's why Bethlehem is called the city of David. Where do you think Joseph had to go? (Bethlehem)

So Joseph and his wife, Mary, prepared for the long journey to Bethlehem. The Bible doesn't tell us how they got to Bethlehem, but they probably walked. Think of walking to [name a place about 70 miles from your town]. **That's how far Joseph and Mary had to travel for this census. And it was even harder because Mary was close to having baby Jesus!**

It took them many days to make this trip. And the biggest surprise was when they finally got to Joseph's hometown of Bethlehem, Mary was ready to have her baby. Jesus was born exactly where God had planned. It was in the little town God told Micah about. Bethlehem.

Use the Clues!
(Bible Review)

■ **Materials:** *Christmas CD/tape, CD/tape player, ball or unbreakable Christmas ornament*

Let's find out what you remember about today's lesson. If you want to add some fun to the review, play a game similar to "Hot Potato." Play music as children pass the ball or ornament. When you randomly stop the music, whoever is holding the object answers a question. For the final round, the one holding the object opens the calendar doors.

■ **What did the prophet Micah say about the Savior's birth?** (he would be born in Bethlehem)

■ **How did God use Caesar Augustus in his plan?** (Augustus called for a census so everyone had to go back to their hometowns to be counted)

■ **Why did Joseph and Mary have to take a trip just before Jesus was born?** (because they had to go to Bethlehem for the census, because <u>God chose Bethlehem for Jesus' birthplace</u>)

■ **What can we trust about God and his plan?** (God makes his plan work out when we follow his ways)

What symbol do you think could stand for what we learned today from the Bible?

Let kids call out ideas. **Choose someone to open door #9. How does a sandal remind us of today's story?** (it reminds us of how far Mary and Joseph walked to Bethlehem)

Let the last child holding the ornament open doors of previous weeks and tell what the symbols stand for.

BIBLE MEMORY WAYPOINT   Deuteronomy 31:8
(Scripture Memory)

■ *Objective: Children will hide God's Word in their hearts for guidance, protection, and encouragement.*

The LORD himself goes before you and will be with you; he will never leave you nor forsake you. Do not be afraid; do not be discouraged (Deuteronomy 31:8).

Read the verse from the poster board. Then have the children read it with you as you point to the words. Divide the class into two (or for large classes, four) groups. Have two groups face each other, with one of them facing the poster to see the verse. The group who can see the verse says the first phrase while the other group echoes it. Continue through the verse. Then have the first group use a different voice (whisper, robot, opera, etc.), which the second group must echo. Change places and repeat twice more with different voices. Then ask if anyone can repeat the verse individually.

PRAYER STATION

■ *Objective: Children will explore and practice prayer for themselves in small groups.*
■ *Materials: copies of StationMaster Card #9 for each adult or teen helper*

Break into small groups of three to five children. Assign a teen or adult helper to each small group and give each helper a copy of *StationMaster Card #9* (see Resources) with ideas for group discussion and prayer.

 ## SNACK STOP: TRAVEL SNACKS

If you plan to provide a snack, this is an ideal time to serve it.

■ *Materials: your choice of trail mix, dried fruit, cheese sticks, cheese crackers, or popcorn*

As children eat, ask them what their favorite snacks are when they go on long trips. Explain that Bible time people had very different foods, such as olives, grapes, dates, milk curds, and pita-like bread.

Note: Always be aware of children with food allergies and have another option on hand if necessary.

 ## APPLICATION

■ *Objective: Children will have opportunities to show how the lesson works in their own lives through activities and take-home papers.*

Some children's ministries may allow children to play outside at this point. If yours does not, choose one of the following activities.

Footsteps to Bethlehem

■ *Materials: brown construction paper, pencils, scissors*

Show children how to trace one of their feet on a sheet of brown paper. After they cut it out, have them work as a group to travel using their paper feet to a place you designate as "Bethlehem." Create a simple but entertaining path to "Bethlehem." They'll lay their feet out end to end to travel along the path, then walk down the foot tracings until they end. Then they'll pick up their feet and repeat until they reach Bethlehem. Try to make the journey a bit winding and arduous to impress on them that Joseph and Mary's trip to Bethlehem was not an easy journey.

Pack Your Bag Relay

■ *Materials: (per team) suitcase or duffel bag, towel, face cloth, pj's, shoes or slippers, hairbrush, toothpaste*

Small classes can do this as one group; the larger the class, the more teams you'll want so everyone gets a chance to participate. Set the suitcases in front of the starting line where the team(s) will begin. At the opposite end of the room, pile up the other items. Children will take turns racing to the pile and choosing one thing to bring back to pack in the suitcase. Add interest by choosing a means of travel, such as hopping, walking backwards, crab walking, skipping, etc. Ask the class what Joseph and Mary might have taken on their trip. If you have students with disabilities, let others help by pushing a wheelchair or by being their "eyes" or "ears."

ON THE FAST TRACK! *(Take-Home Papers)*

Reward children that brought back signed tickets with a trip to the treasure box. **I'm going to hand out your *On the Fast Track!* papers now. Don't forget to do the activities and learn the verse. There's a crossword puzzle this week that will help you remember some of the things we've talked about so far.**

Distribute the take-home papers and paper feet (if made) just before children leave.

LESSON TEN: Angelic Invitation

Angels and Shepherds

Memory Verse:
You make me glad by your deeds, O LORD; I sing for joy at the works of your hands (Psalm 92:4).

Bible Basis:
Luke 2:8–20

Bible Truth:
Angels invite the shepherds to worship Jesus.

You Will Need:

- [ ] Celebration Calendar
- [ ] 1 poster board
- [ ] Bible time dress-up box
- [ ] baby doll
- [ ] soft cloths or a towel
- [ ] *On the Fast Track! #10* take-home paper
- [ ] *StationMaster Card #10*
- [ ] (optional) treasure box
- [ ] (optional) snack: large pretzel rods or bread-sticks, honey (optional)
- [ ] (optional) Activity #2: Advent wreath, four purple or pink candles, one white candle, matches, purple and yellow paper, scissors, glue sticks, rulers

When you see this icon, it means preparation will take more than five minutes.

GET SET!
(Lesson Preparation)

- Print today's Bible memory verse on a poster board: **You make me glad by your deeds, O LORD; I sing for joy at the works of your hands (Psalm 92:4).**
- Make a copy of *On the Fast Track! #10* take-home paper for each child.
- Make a copy of *StationMaster Card #10* for each helper.
- If using Activity #1, prepare the Advent wreath by inserting and securing four purple candles around the circle and the white one in the middle.
- Create a purple candle bookmark sample if using it in Activity #2.
- Set out Celebration Calendar and (optional) treasure box.
- Set up snack and outside play activities if you include these items in your children's ministry.

TICKETS PLEASE!
(Welcome and Bible Connection)

- **Objective:** *To excite children's interest and connect their own life experiences with the Bible Truth, children will focus on shepherds by playing "Follow the Leader."*

Welcome Time Activity: Follow Me

Sheep are known for their instinct to follow the leader of the herd. As children arrive, have them join a helper and other children where the helper is leading a game of "Follow the Leader."

Sharing Time and Bible Connection

When everyone has arrived, call children to the lesson area and welcome them. Introduce today's lesson with the following activity. As you talk, give every child the opportunity to say something.

Let's find out what you already know about shepherds. I'm going to say some things about shepherds in Bible times. If you agree with what I say, stand up. If you don't agree, stay sitting down.

- **Shepherds had important jobs.** (agree)
- **Shepherds earned lots of money for watching sheep.** (disagree)
- **Being a shepherd could be a lonely job.** (agree)
- **Shepherds had to sleep with their herd of sheep.** (agree)
- **Being a shepherd was a very safe job. (**disagree)
- **Shepherds got pretty dirty out in the field and didn't get to take hot baths or showers.** (agree)

Hey, you already know some things about shepherds. Even though these men had dirty and tiring jobs, God gave them a special opportunity when the Savior was born. Let's hear just what happened to them one night.

 # ALL ABOARD FOR BIBLE TRUTH   Luke 2:8–20
(Bible Discover and Learn Time)

- *Objective: Children will study Luke 2:8–20 and learn how angels invited the shepherds to worship the newborn Jesus.*
- *Materials: Bible time dress-up box, baby doll, soft cloths or a towel*

Today, we're going to learn the Bible story directly from the Bible. While I read it, you'll act it out. If desired, children can choose some clothes and props from the dress-up box. Choose a Mary and Joseph. Give them the doll and cloths and send them to the back of the room to wait for their part. Half of the remaining children will act as shepherds; the other half will be angels. Ask angels to move to one side to await their part.

This story is from the book of Luke. Read from Luke 2:8: **"And there were shepherds living out in the fields nearby, keeping watch over their flocks at night,"** Shepherds can shield their eyes with a hand as if looking for their flocks on one side of the room and then another. **"An angel of the Lord appeared to them, and the glory of the Lord shone around them,"** Have one angel wave his or her arms. **"and they were terrified."** Shepherds cower in terror. **"But the angel said to them, 'Do not be afraid. I bring you good news of great joy that will be for all the people. Today in the town of David a Savior has been born to you; he is Christ the Lord. This will be a sign to you: You will find a baby wrapped in cloths and lying in a manger.'"** Shepherds should look at each other with amazement and bewildered expressions.

"Suddenly a great company of the heavenly host appeared with the angel," All the angels stand around the first angel and wave their arms. **"praising God and saying, 'Glory to God in the highest, and on earth peace to men on whom his favor rests.'"** Angels can say, "Glory to God in the highest," a few times.

Angels leave. **"When the angels had left them and gone into heaven, the shepherds said to one another, 'Let's go to Bethlehem and see this thing that has happened, which the Lord has told us about.'"** Shepherds pretend to talk to each other.

"So they hurried off," Shepherds scurry from the front to the back of the room where Joseph and Mary are waiting. **"and found Mary and Joseph, and the baby, who was lying in the manger. When they had seen him, they spread the word concerning what had been told them about this child,"** Shepherds spread out and pretend to tell people about the baby. **"and all who heard it were amazed at what the shepherds said to them."**

"But Mary treasured up all these things and pondered them in her heart." Mary can smile and nod. Shepherds go back to where they started. **"The shepherds returned, glorifying and praising God for all the things they had heard and seen, which were just as they had been told."**

Give appreciation to children for their efforts.

The story of the shepherds is so surprising. Of all the people God could have told this exciting news to first, he chose some shepherds. <u>God used angels to invite the shepherds to be the first to worship the Messiah and Savior.</u>

Worshipping Jesus wasn't something just for those shepherds. It's how you and I show our love and honor to Jesus now. When we praise him, sing to him, pray and give him our attention, we're following the shepherds' example of worship.

Use the Clues!
(Bible Review)

Let's talk about today's lesson.

- **How did the shepherds find out about the birth of Jesus?** (angels gave them the news)
- **What did the angels invite the shepherds to do?** (find the baby and worship him)
- **What did the shepherds do with this invitation?** (they went right away and worshipped him)
- **How are the shepherds an example for you and me?** (we should worship Jesus like the shepherds did)

What symbol do you think could stand for what we learned today from the Bible? Let kids call out ideas. Choose someone to open door #10. **How does a sheep remind us of today's story?** (it makes us think of the shepherds who the angels invited to be the first to worship Jesus)

Choose a volunteer to open doors of previous weeks and tell what the symbols stand for.

BIBLE MEMORY WAYPOINT   Psalm 92:4
(Scripture Memory)

- ***Objective:*** *Children will hide God's Word in their hearts for guidance, protection, and encouragement.*

You make me glad by your deeds, O LORD; I sing for joy at the works of your hands (Psalm 92:4).

Read this week's memory verse from the poster, pointing to each word as you do. To help children learn the Bible verse, they will play the "Arm Link Game." Practice the verse several times to familiarize the children with it. Then have the children stand around the room. The children will "bind" together by linking arms and saying the verse together. First, the chidren will walk randomly around the room, saying the verse. Then, at your signal, each child links arms with another child, and the pairs say the verse. Give another signal. Each pair links arms with another pair, and these new groups repeat the verse. Continue playing the game until all the children in the room are linked together.

PRAYER STATION

- **Objective:** *Children will explore and practice prayer for themselves in small groups.*
- **Materials:** *copies of* StationMaster Card #10 *for each adult or teen helper*

Break into small groups of three to five children. Assign a teen or adult helper to each small group and give each helper a copy of *StationMaster Card #10* (see Resources) with ideas for group discussion and prayer.

 ## SNACK STOP: TASTY SHEPHERD'S STAFF (Optional)

If you plan to provide a snack, this is an ideal time to serve it.

- **Materials:** *large pretzel rods or breadsticks, honey (optional)*

Hand out the pretzels and breadsticks. If desired, you can offer children the option of dipping their pretzels or breadsticks in honey.

As children munch on their shepherd's staff, engage them in discussion about how a shepherd used a staff and crook to help him with the sheep. Ask children how the shepherd might have used the staff. (for walking on uneven or rocky ground, to guide sheep in the right direction, or to fight against predators)

Note: Always be aware of children with food allergies and have another option on hand if necessary.

APPLICATION

- **Objective:** *Children will have opportunities to show how the lesson works in their own lives through activities and take-home papers.*

Some children's ministries may allow children to play outside at this point. If yours does not, choose one of the following activities.

 **Shepherds and Sheep Tag**

Divide your class into groups of three to four. Choose a wolf, a sheep, and several shepherds. Shepherds will join hands with the sheep and form a small circle. The wolf will stand outside the circle and try to tag the sheep. The shepherds will spin the circle around (without letting go) and try to keep the wolf away from the sheep. If the wolf tags the sheep, players exchange roles and play again.

 The Advent Wreath and Candles

■ *Materials: Advent wreath with five candles, matches, purple and yellow paper, scissors, glue sticks, rulers*

The four Sundays before Christmas are a celebration called Advent. Advent means waiting for something important. It's a time to think about the coming of Jesus. Today and the next three weeks, we'll participate in Advent by lighting one new candle each week. Light one purple candle. **The first candle in the Advent wreath reminds us of hope. What prophet told people that Jesus would come one day?** (Isaiah) **This candle stands for the hope the prophets' messages gave, the hope for eternal life when the Savior came**.

If desired, hand out purple and yellow construction paper. Students will trace a ruler to draw a long purple candle. They can cut out a small yellow flame to glue to the top. Have them write "Messiah, Savior, Jesus" on the candle. Encourage them to use these as bookmarks to remind them of God's plan that was fulfilled in Jesus.

Blow out the candle when this activity is finished.

 ON THE FAST TRACK! *(Take-Home Papers)*

Collect tickets from children who completed last week's take-home work and let them choose something from the treasure box. **Thank you for finishing your take-home papers and bringing in your tickets. Don't forget to do the same this week!** Ask a child to help you hand out *On the Fast Track! #10*. **I can't wait to see how many of you bring back signed tickets next week!**

If the children made the candle bookmarks, distribute them before children leave.

LESSON ELEVEN: Call Him Jesus

Anna and Simeon

Memory Verse:

The heavens proclaim his righteousness, and all the peoples see his glory (Psalm 97:6).

Bible Basis:

Luke 2:21–38

Bible Truth:

The righteous recognize and honor Jesus.

You Will Need:

- ☐ Celebration Calendar
- ☐ 1 poster board
- ☐ 15 common classroom and household items in a bag or box
- ☐ extra bag or box
- ☐ a baby picture of yourself, something you drew or created as a child or young person, current photo of yourself
- ☐ Bible time dress-up box
- ☐ baby doll and blanket
- ☐ ball or beanbag
- ☐ *On the Fast Track! #11* take-home paper
- ☐ *StationMaster Card #11*
- ☐ *(optional)* treasure box
- ☐ *(optional)* snack: trail mix or cereal O's and sunflower seed kernels
- ☐ *(optional)* Activity #1: Advent wreath with four purple or pink candles and one white candle, matches, 15" x 4" paper strips, scissors, glitter glue, tape, pencils

 When you see this icon, it means preparation will take more than five minutes.

 GET SET!
(Lesson Preparation)

- ■ Print today's Bible memory verse on a poster board: **The heavens proclaim his righteousness, and all the peoples see his glory (Psalm 97:6).**
- ■ Make a copy of *On the Fast Track! #11* for each helper.
- ■ Make a copy of *StationMaster Card #11* for each helper.
- ■ Set out the Celebration Calendar and *(optional)* treasure box.
- ■ Set up snack and outside play activities if you include these items in your children's ministry.
- ■ Cut 15" x 4" paper strips for each child if using Activity #1.

 TICKETS PLEASE!
(Welcome and Bible Connection)

- ■ *Objective: To excite children's interest and connect their own life experiences with the Bible Truth, children will play a game of recognition.*

Welcome Time Activity: Name That Thing

■ *Materials: 15 common small classroom and household items in a bag or box, extra bag or box*

As children arrive, send them to the table where a helper is playing a game with the children. The helper will choose one item from the collection and make a big deal about secretly getting it into the empty box. Then each child will have a short time (10 seconds) to feel the item with one or both hands without looking. After everyone has had a chance to touch the item, the helper will ask, "Do you recognize this item?" Kids can raise their hands to guess it. After someone correctly guesses the item, repeat the process with a new item. Throughout this game, focus on recognition.

Sharing Time and Bible Connection

■ *Materials: a baby picture of yourself, something you drew or created as a child or young person, current photo of yourself*

When everyone has arrived, call children to the lesson area and welcome them. As you move into discussion to prepare for the Bible story, give every child the opportunity to say something.

Look around at the other people in our class. Do you see anyone you don't recognize? If so, ask that person his or her name. Give a moment for this to happen. **Now if you see anyone from the class later today at the park or a store, you'll recognize each other.**

■ **Now let's see if you can recognize someone else. The person looked like this as a baby.** Show your baby picture. **Do you recognize this person?**
■ **The person made this picture.** Show your childhood artwork. **Do you recognize him or her?**
■ **This person grew up in** [name your hometown or state]. **Do you know who it is?**
■ **And this person's middle name is** [your middle name]. **Do you recognize the person?**
■ **Here's what the person looks like today.** Show current photo of yourself. **Now who is this person?**

Good! All of you eventually recognized me. A couple of centuries ago, an old man from Bible times was waiting to recognize someone he had been waiting for. But he'd never seen this person. So how would he know who it was? That's what we're about to find out in our story today.

ALL ABOARD FOR BIBLE TRUTH

(Bible Discover and Learn Time)

Luke 2:21-38

- ■ *Objective:* Children will study Luke 2:21–38 and discover how two godly, righteous people recognized the baby Jesus and honored him.
- ■ *Materials:* Bible time dress-up box, baby doll and blanket

Last week we discovered that when Jesus was born, God announced his birth by sending lots of angels to tell the shepherds this news. Then the shepherds worshipped the baby because he was God. After Jesus was born, his parents followed some Jewish traditions. When he was eight days old, they named him Jesus, just like God had told them to do. Then they took their little boy to the temple to present him. The parents had to offer a sacrifice of two turtledoves or two pigeons.

But two very unusual and surprising things happened while Mary and Joseph were at the temple. Have two boys and two girls choose clothes from the dress-up box. Set up a freeze frame of one boy as Simeon holding the doll while a boy and girl as Joseph and Mary watch, surprised. **An old man came right up to the parents and took the baby!** We might think that was a little strange today, but in Bible times old people were very respected and honored. This man was Simeon, and God had spoken to him. God had told Simeon that he would see the Savior before he died. So every day Simeon waited at the temple and watched. That day, when Mary and Joseph brought their newborn into the temple, Simeon recognized him. It was Jesus! Wow!

Here's what is says in Luke 2 about Simeon recognizing Jesus. Ask one or two volunteers to read Luke 2:28–32. **How do you think Mary and Joseph felt?** (amazed, surprised, shocked, excited) **The Bible says they were amazed.**

Simeon blessed them and told them that Jesus would have an influence on many people. Simeon actor can sit down. **Then another person who recognized the baby as the Savior came up to Mary and Joseph.** Set up second freeze frame with the second girl as Anna, standing in front of Mary and Joseph with her face lifted to heaven and hands held as if in prayer.

This woman was named Anna. She was 84 years old, and had also been waiting for the birth of the Messiah and Savior. She walked right up to the parents and baby. Here's what Luke said that she did. Ask another volunteer to read Luke 2:38. **Anna recognized that this little boy was the One God had sent, the One the Jews had been waiting for for centuries. It was another amazing moment for Mary and Joseph.** All freeze frame actors can sit down.

When you were born, your parents and other people in your family got to know you really quickly. They could recognize you by the way you cried, or yawned, or made a funny face. Anna and Simeon had never seen Jesus. They had no clue what the Messiah and Savior would look like. But God's Spirit told them when Mary and Joseph brought

their baby into the temple that this was the One. <u>They recognized God's voice and they recognized the Savior</u>. **How do you and I recognize Jesus with us today?** (we recognize is teachings in the Bible, we pray and listen for him)

Use the Clues!
(Bible Review)

■ *Materials: ball or beanbag*
What do you remember about the lesson? Let's see. Toss a ball or beanbag to a child and ask the child to answer the question. If he/she can do so, he/she gets to toss the ball to another child. If the child can't answer, he/she throws it back to you and you toss it to a different person.

■ **What traditions did Mary and Joseph follow after Jesus was born?** (naming him, presenting him at the temple and offering a sacrifice)

■ **How did Simeon recognize the Savior when He was just a baby?** (God's spirit told him that Jesus was the One he was waiting for)

■ **How did Anna show she recognized Jesus?** (she walked up to them and began thanking God and telling people about Jesus)

■ **How would we recognize God today?** (we recognize his teachings in the Bible, we pray and listen for him)

What symbol do you think could stand for what we learned today from the Bible? Let kids call out ideas. Choose someone to open door #11. **This is a picture of a temple. How can the temple remind us of today's story?** (it reminds us of the temple where Mary and Joseph took Jesus)

Choose a volunteer to open doors of previous weeks and tell what the symbols stand for.

BIBLE MEMORY WAYPOINT
(Scripture Memory)   Psalm 97:6

■ *Objective: Children will hide God's Word in their hearts for guidance, protection, and encouragement.*

The heavens proclaim his righteousness, and all the peoples see his glory (Psalm 97:6).

Read the verse from the poster, and then have the children slowly read it with you as you point to the words. Ask the children to get into pairs. A helper can pair up with a child if the group is an uneven number. Explain that the pairs will help each other memorize the verse. One person will say the first part and the other person will say the second. They can repeat the reference together. Everyone should be able to see the verse on the board. Practice together as a large group, then let the children work in their pairs to memorize.

PRAYER STATION

- ■ **Objective:** *Children will explore and practice prayer for themselves in small groups.*
- ■ **Materials:** *copies of* StationMaster Card #11 *for each adult or teen helper*

Break into groups of three to five children. Assign a teen or adult helper to each small group and give each helper a copy of *StationMaster Card #11* (see Resources) with ideas for group discussion and prayer.

SNACK STOP: PIGEON FOOD (Optional)

If you plan to provide a snack, this is an ideal time to serve it.

- ■ **Materials:** *trail mix or cereal O's and sunflower seed kernels*

Hand out the snack to the children. Comment on how the trail mix or cereal O's and sunflower seeds look a little like bird food. Ask children what birds eat. (bird seed, plant seeds, bugs) Discuss how Mary and Joseph took turtledoves or pigeons to the temple to offer as a sacrifice. This was the custom before Jesus died for our sins. People had to give a blood offering for their sins to be removed. They knew that this was a result of the sin committed in the Garden of Eden. It wasn't until Jesus died on the cross as the perfect offering that God no longer required blood sacrifices.

Note: Always be aware of children with food allergies and have another option on hand if necessary.

APPLICATION

- ■ **Objective:** *Children will have opportunities to show how the lesson works in their own lives through activities and take-home papers.*

Some children's ministries may allow children to play outside at this point. If yours does not, choose one of the following activities.

Advent Wreath

■ *Materials: Advent wreath, four purple or pink candles, one white candle, matches, 15" x 4" paper strips, scissors, pencils, glitter glue, tape*

Light the candle used last week. **What does this first candle stand for in our Advent wreath?** (hope) **It reminds us of the hope people had as they waited for the prophecies about the Messiah and Savior to come true. The second purple candle is for peace. The angels who announced Jesus' birth to the shepherds said Jesus would bring peace on earth. And peace is one of Jesus' names that Isaiah wrote about. What was that name?** (Prince of Peace) Light the second purple or pink candle. **As we wait for the day we'll celebrate Jesus' birth, we can look forward to the peace he'll bring to the world one day.**

If desired, let children make a "curly crown." Give each child a 15" x 4" paper strip and scissors. Show children how to cut a fringe into one of the long edges of the paper, so that each piece of fringe is about 1" wide. Then, roll fringe around a pencil, one strand at a time, so that when released, the strands are curly. Decorate crowns with glitter glue. Wait until crowns are dry to tape into a circle for children to wear, curly side out. If not dry, send home flat. Extinguish candles when the activity is finished.

Tradition Charades

Review from the Bible story what Jewish traditions Mary and Joseph observed after Jesus' birth. (naming, presenting him at the temple, offering a sacrifice) Have children think up a Christmas tradition we observe and act it out without using words. Let others guess what it is. If you have a large group, you can divide into separate groups so more kids have a chance to pantomime. Be ready with some suggestions of Christmas traditions if children come up blank.

ON THE FAST TRACK! *(Take-Home Papers)*

Collect tickets from children who completed last week's take-home work and let them choose something from the treasure box. **This week's take-home activity is fun! Be sure to ask your parents to sign your ticket after you complete the activity. That way, you can choose a prize from the treasure box when you bring the tickets back to me next week.**

Distribute the take-home papers and crowns (if made) just before children leave.

LESSON TWELVE: A Gift from Heaven

The Magi

Memory Verse:

From infancy you have known **the holy Scriptures, which are able to make you wise for salvation through faith in Christ Jesus** (2 Timothy 3:15).

*Early elementary verse in **bold** type.*

Bible Basis:

Matthew 2:1–3, 7–12

Bible Truth:

Wise men worship Jesus.

You Will Need:

- [ ] Celebration Calendar
- [ ] 1 poster board
- [ ] butcher paper
- [ ] large index cards or card stock
- [ ] homemade map
- [ ] *On the Fast Track!* #12 take-home paper
- [ ] *StationMaster Card* #12
- [ ] (*optional*) treasure box
- [ ] (*optional*) snack: decorated Christmas or sugar cookies, juice
- [ ] (*optional*) Activity #1: Advent wreath, four purple or pink candles, one white candle, matches, CD/tape of "O Come All Ye Faithful," CD/tape player or guitar/piano
- [ ] (*optional*) Activity #2: male doll or paper Jesus

 When you see this icon, it means preparation will take more than five minutes.

 GET SET!
(Lesson Preparation)

- ◉ Print today's Bible memory verse on a poster board: **From infancy you have known the holy Scriptures, which are able to make you wise for salvation through faith in Christ Jesus** (2 Timothy 3:15).
- ◉ Print each portion of Bible text from Matthew (*see All Aboard section*) on separate large index cards. Number cards from 1 to 18 in one corner.
- Make a simple map that leads from your classroom to a place in the church such as the drinking fountain, nursery, kitchen or main sanctuary.
- Make a copy of *On the Fast Track!* #12 take-home paper for each child.
- Make a copy of *StationMaster Card* #12 for each helper.
- Set out Celebration Calendar and (*optional*) treasure box.
- Set up snack and outside play activities if you include these items in your children's ministry.

 TICKETS PLEASE!
(Welcome and Bible Connection)

- **Objective:** *To excite children's interest and connect their own life experiences with the Bible Truth, children will design maps to a common location.*

Welcome Time Activity: Map Making

■ *Materials: butcher paper, pencils*
Choose one or two places in the church that the children would be familiar with such as the sanctuary, drinking fountain, or playground. Let them draw a map on paper or write directions on how to reach that location from the classroom where they are. Helpers or older students can work with younger children.

Sharing Time and Bible Connection

When everyone has arrived, call children to the lesson area and welcome them. Introduce today's lesson with the following activity. As you talk, give every child the opportunity to say something.

Show children a map made during the Welcome Time Activity or your own home-made map.

■ **Where do you think this map will lead us?** If practical, ask a child to use the map to lead the class to the location. If not, pass the map around and let children figure out where it leads.

■ **When have you seen people using maps?** (to go on vacation, driving in a new town, to locate a specific business or park, etc.)

■ **What other sorts of ways do people find a place they've never been?** (the Internet, ask directions from someone who knows, randomly roam around)

■ **How would someone back in Jesus' time have found a new place?** (ask someone who's been there, use landmarks)

In Bible times, some important men traveled a long way to visit with the Christ child. But near the end of their journey they got a little lost. Let's find out where they got directions.

ALL ABOARD FOR BIBLE TRUTH

Matthew 2:1-3, 7-12

(Bible Discover and Learn Time)

■ *Objective: Children will study Matthew 2:1–3, 7–12 to learn about the wise men who persisted until they found Jesus.*
■ *Materials: Bible text printed on index cards or card stock*

Our Bible study today is going to be a group effort. Each of you will tell a part of the story. For large classes of more than 18 children, have kids pair up with one good

reader in each pair. For classes with less than 18 children, some or all kids will have more than one card.

Hand out story cards to children; they can stand in a semicircle in order of the card number they are holding. Before starting, you and helpers can read each child's card with him or her so they understand what to read. Helpers can stand ready to assist younger children as needed. Encourage children to use dramatic voices if they are speaking a part of the wise men or Herod.

Let's tell the story as a class. Read your part of the story loud and clear.

Card 1: Jesus was born in Bethlehem.

Card 2: Herod was the king in Jerusalem.

Card 3: Wise men called magi came from the east to Jerusalem.

Card 4: They asked, "Where is the king of the Jews?"

Card 5: "We saw his star."

Card 6: "We want to worship the new king."

Card 7: King Herod was worried. Who was this other king?

Card 8: King Herod sent the wise men to Bethlehem.

Card 9: King Herod said, "Come back to see me soon."

Card 10: "Tell me when you find the child. I want to worship him too."

Card 11: The wise men went to Bethlehem.

Card 12: They found the star above a house.

Card 13: They found Mary and Jesus in the house.

Card 14: They worshipped Jesus and gave him precious gifts.

Card 15: They gave Jesus gold, incense, and myrrh.

Card 16: God warned the wise men in a dream about King Herod.

Card 17: God said not to go back to King Herod.

Card 18: **They went back to their own country by another road.**

When the story is finished, congratulate your students for telling the Bible story so well. Let them applaud each other.

Use the Clues!
(Bible Review)

Let's find out what you remember about today's lesson.

- **Who were the two kings in the story?** (Jesus and Herod)
- **Why were the wise men looking for Jesus?** (they had seen his star and wanted to worship him)
- **How did the <u>wise men honor and worship Jesus</u>?** (they gave him wonderful gifts)

- **What are some things about the wise men that are good examples for us?** (they honored Jesus as a king, they didn't give up looking for him, they listened to God in a dream)

What symbol do you think could stand for what we learned today from the Bible? Let kids call out ideas. Choose someone to open door #12. **How does a wrapped gift remind us of today's story?** (it's a reminder of the wise men who were persistent until they found Jesus and could give him their gifts and worship)

Choose a volunteer to open doors of previous weeks and tell what the symbols stand for.

BIBLE MEMORY WAYPOINT
(Scripture Memory)

2 Timothy 3:15

- ***Objective:*** *Children will hide God's Word in their hearts for guidance, protection, and encouragement.*

From infancy you have known the holy Scriptures, which are able to make you wise for salvation through faith in Christ Jesus (2 Timothy 3:15).

Read the verse from the poster, then read it again slowly with the children as you point to the words. To help them commit the verse to memory, have the children line up or form a circle. Call out a category; whoever fits that category steps forward and reads/says the verse in unison. Do this five or six times until the verse becomes familiar. Categories can include hair color, girls/boys, blue clothing, birthday months, etc.

PRAYER STATION

- **Objective:** *Children will explore and practice prayer for themselves in small groups.*
- **Materials:** *copies of* StationMaster Card #12 *for each adult or teen helper*

Break into small groups of three to five children. Assign a teen or adult helper to each small group and give each helper a copy of *StationMaster Card #12* (see Resources) with ideas for group discussion and prayer.

SNACK STOP: KINGLY FEAST (Optional)

If you plan to provide a snack, this is an ideal time to serve it.

- **Materials:** *decorated Christmas or sugar cookies, juice*

Ask children what kinds of foods they might eat as a special feast given for a king. Tell them you brought something special for them today. As children eat their decorated treats, discuss how the wise men must have felt to eat in King Herod's palace after traveling for a long time.

Note: Always be aware of children with food allergies and have another option on hand if necessary.

APPLICATION

- **Objective:** *Children will have opportunities to show how the lesson works in their own lives through activities and take-home papers.*

Some children's ministries may allow children to play outside at this point. If yours does not, choose one of the following activities.

Advent Wreath

■ *Materials: Advent wreath, four purple or pink candles, one white candle, matches, CD/tape of "O Come All Ye Faithful," CD/tape player or guitar/piano*

As you light the first two candles, ask what they represent. (hope and peace) **This week we're lighting the candle that stands for joy. Knowing Jesus is coming to be our Messiah and Savior is a huge reason to be joyful. What does it mean to have joy?** (to be very happy about something) **As we light this candle, we're getting closer to what we're waiting for—the celebration of Jesus' birth!** Light the third candle.

Use background music, a live instrument, or sing a capella the chorus, "O come let us adore him" from the song, "O Come All Ye Faithful." After one time through with the traditional words, try using these words: "We wait for you, rejoicing; we wait for you, rejoicing; we wait for you, rejoicing, Christ the Lord."

Blow out the candle when this activity is finished.

 Find the King!

■ *Materials: male doll or paper Jesus*

Hide a doll or paper Jesus in the classroom. Children will pretend to be the wise men and look for Jesus. Once the doll is found, let the one who found it hide the doll again. Add another element to the hunt by appointing someone to be King Herod. Move furniture to the sides of the room, and then have Herod try to tag children as they hunt for Jesus. Once a student is tagged, the tagged one sits out until the doll is hidden the next time. Ask the children to think of some hardships that the wise men might have experienced as they searched for Jesus.

 ON THE FAST TRACK! *(Take-Home Papers)*

Thanks for bringing your tickets today. Allow children that brought a signed ticket to choose a prize from the treasure box. If any of the children did not bring tickets, remind them that they will be able to choose a prize when they complete the activities and bring their signed tickets to class next week.

Distribute the take-home papers. **Have fun doing the activities this week. I hope everyone has a ticket for me next time.**

LESSON THIRTEEN: Happy Birthday, Jesus!

Memory Verse:

The Word became flesh and made his dwelling among us. We have seen his glory, the glory of the One and Only, who came from the Father, full of grace and truth **(John 1:14).**

*Early elementary verse in **bold** type.*

Bible Basis:
Luke 2:6–7

Bible Truth:
God keeps his promise.

You Will Need:

- [ ] Celebration Calendar
- [ ] 1 poster board
- [ ] balloons
- [ ] streamers
- [ ] permanent markers
- [ ] Advent wreath
- [ ] four purple and one white candle
- [ ] matches
- [ ] nativity set
- [ ] butcher paper
- [ ] (optional) treats such as Christmas pencils or erasers, mini candy canes, etc.
- [ ] gift-wrapped box
- [ ] *On the Fast Track! #13* take-home paper
- [ ] *StationMaster Card #13*
- [ ] (optional) treasure box
- [ ] (optional) snack: birthday cake, milk or juice, plates, plastic forks, cups, birthday napkins, birthday candles, matches
- [ ] (optional) Activity #1: card stock, glitter glue, crayons, and other decorating supplies; optional: shrink plastic, markers, baking sheet(s)
- [ ] (optional) Activity #2: birthday supplies from Snack Stop, Advent wreath and candles, matches

 GET SET!
(Lesson Preparation)

- ■ Print the verse in short phrases in large print on card stock strips, 3–5 words per strip. Pin to a bulletin board within eye level of the children, or tape to a wall at eye level. **The Word became flesh and made his dwelling among us. We have seen his glory, the glory of the One and Only, who came from the Father, full of grace and truth (John 1:14).**
- ■ Make a copy of *On the Fast Track! #13* take-home paper for each child.
- ■ Make a copy of *StationMaster Card #13* for each helper.
- ■ Set out the Celebration Calendar and *(optional)* treasure box.
- ■ Set up snack or outside play activities if you include these items in your children's ministry.

 When you see this icon, it means preparation will take more than five minutes.

TICKETS PLEASE!
(Welcome and Bible Connection)

■ **Objective:** *To excite children's interest and connect their own life experiences with the Bible Truth, children will create decorations for Jesus' birthday party.*

Welcome Time Activity: Party Preparations

■ **Materials:** *balloons, permanent markers, streamers, scissors, paper, markers*
Let arriving children begin making decorations for the birthday party for Jesus. They can blow up balloons and draw or write on them with permanent markers, cut streamers and tape to chairs, doors, bulletin boards, etc. Helpers can assist children by tying off the inflated balloons, if necessary.

Sharing Time and Bible Connection

■ **Materials:** *Advent wreath, candles, matches*

When everyone has arrived, call children to the lesson area and welcome them. Light the three previously lit candles on the Advent wreath and ask children to tell you what they stand for. (hope, peace, joy) **The last purple/pink candle stands for love. God loved you and me and all people so much he wanted to give us a way for our sins to be forgiven. So he sent our Messiah and Savior, Jesus. That's what we've been waiting for.** Light the last purple or pink candle. **There's just one candle left—the white one—and we'll light it later today.**

■ **What do you think this last candle is about?** If no one knows, don't tell them yet.
■ **What event has Advent been leading us to?** (Christmas, the celebration of Jesus' birth)
■ **How do you celebrate your birthday?** (with parties, presents, special meals, cards)

We're going to find out how God kept his promise and fulfilled his plan. And we'll be able to celebrate today!

ALL ABOARD FOR BIBLE TRUTH   Luke 2:6–7
(Bible Discover and Learn Time)

■ *Objective:* Children will study Luke 2:6–7 to discover the reason we celebrate on Christmas.

■ *Materials:* nativity set, party supplies made in Welcome Time Activity or prepared in advance, butcher paper, crayons or markers

How do you feel on your birthday and when it's time for a party? What kinds of feelings do you have? (excitement, can't wait, fun) **That's why we have such a good reason to celebrate Jesus' birthday. His coming was even more important than your birth or mine. The day Jesus was born was the day God's promises and plan came true. How long did people wait for the Messiah and Savior to arrive?** (hundreds of years) **After all that waiting, their desires came true.**

Point to the nativity set. **Let's share the way God planned and made Jesus' birthday happen by using these figures to recreate the story.** Hand out the figures from the nativity set, asking children one by one to place their figure on the table to create the birthday of Jesus. As they add their piece, each child will tell what part that individual played in the story. Place Mary, Joseph, and Jesus last.

There are some people we learned about who aren't in this nativity scene. Who can you think of? (Simeon, Anna, John the Baptist, Herod) **All of these people had a part in the story of Jesus' coming. And you and I are a part, too, because Jesus was born on earth to be your Savior and mine.**

Let's set up our party to celebrate Jesus' birthday! If not already done during the Welcome Time Activity, let children decorate with balloons and streamers. They can also create a birthday banner on butcher paper by writing "Happy Birthday, Jesus." Make the Advent wreath part of the decorations on the table where you'll have the cake. You can have the actual party now, or during the Application time. The plan for the party is under Application Activity #1.

Use the Clues!
(Bible Review)

■ *Materials:* (optional) treats such as Christmas pencils or erasers, mini candy canes, etc.

Review the past 12 weeks of Bible stories using the Celebration Calendar. If desired, offer small treats when children correctly identify the symbol with the story it represents. Give all children a chance to win a treat by having different children tell main parts of the stories.

BIBLE MEMORY WAYPOINT
(Scripture Memory)

John 1:14

- **Objective:** *Children will hide God's Word in their hearts for guidance, protection, and encouragement.*
- **Materials:** *verse phrases on card stock strips which are mounted on the board, gift-wrapped box*

The Word became flesh and made his dwelling among us. We have seen his glory, the glory of the One and Only, who came from the Father, full of grace and truth (John 1:14).

Read the verse from the card stock strips. Then have children read it with you as you point to the words. Explain confusing words or terms, such as "became flesh" and "One and Only." Take down the strips and toss them in mixed-up order in the gift-wrapped box. Have children each take out a strip and work with each other to put the phrases back in correct order. Recite the completed verse together, and then repeat the activity.

PRAYER STATION

- **Objective:** *Children will explore and practice prayer for themselves in small groups.*
- **Materials:** *copies of* StationMaster Card #13 *for each adult or teen helper*

Break into small groups of three to five children. Assign a teen or adult helper to each small group and give each helper a copy of *StationMaster Card #13* (see Resources) with ideas for group discussion and prayer.

SNACK STOP: BIRTHDAY PARTY (Optional)

If you plan to provide a snack, integrate it this week with the Map Presentation and Party as suggested below.

■ *Materials:* *birthday cake, milk or juice, plates, plastic forks, cups, birthday napkins, birthday candles, matches*

Mesh the snack time with your birthday party, either during the Bible story time or Activity #1.

Note: Always be aware of children with food allergies and have another option on hand if necessary.

 # APPLICATION

■ *Objective:* *To celebrate with children not only their accomplishments as they've searched for God in every circumstance of life, but also their discovery of the great treasure of God's relentless pursuit of each precious child.*

Some children's ministries may allow children to play outside at this point. If yours does not, choose one of the following activities.

Thank You Cards

■ **Materials:** *card stock, glitter glue, crayons, and other decorating supplies; optional: shrink plastic, markers, baking sheet(s)*

Let children create thank you cards to Jesus for coming to earth and becoming their Savior. Allow them to use the glitter glue, stamps, and crayons to decorate their cards and write a thank you message to Jesus. If you have access to a craft store that sells shrink plastic, allow kids to create their own Christmas ornaments on the plastic and write a thank you message to Jesus on the ornament. If possible, bake the shrink plastic pieces in the church oven.

Birthday Party

■ **Materials:** *birthday cake and juice from Snack Stop, Advent wreath and candles, matches.*

Use the Advent wreath as the center-piece decoration for the party, along with the cake. Light the white candle. **This candle stands for Jesus. He came to be the Light of the world. His coming changed everyone's life because he brought us forgiveness for our sins. So instead of receiving gifts for his birthday, he gave us a gift!**
Lead the children in singing "Happy Birthday" to Jesus, then give thanks for his birth that gave us life. Enjoy the cake together.

ON THE FAST TRACK! *(Take-Home Papers)*

If you have a signed ticket, please bring it to me. Let kids who brought a signed ticket pick out a treat from the treasure box.

Even though this is the last week of the unit, remind kids to do the activities on the take-home paper and bring their signed tickets next time the class meets.

Distribute the take-home papers and thank you art, if made, just before children leave.

**Celebration
Cake
Calendar**

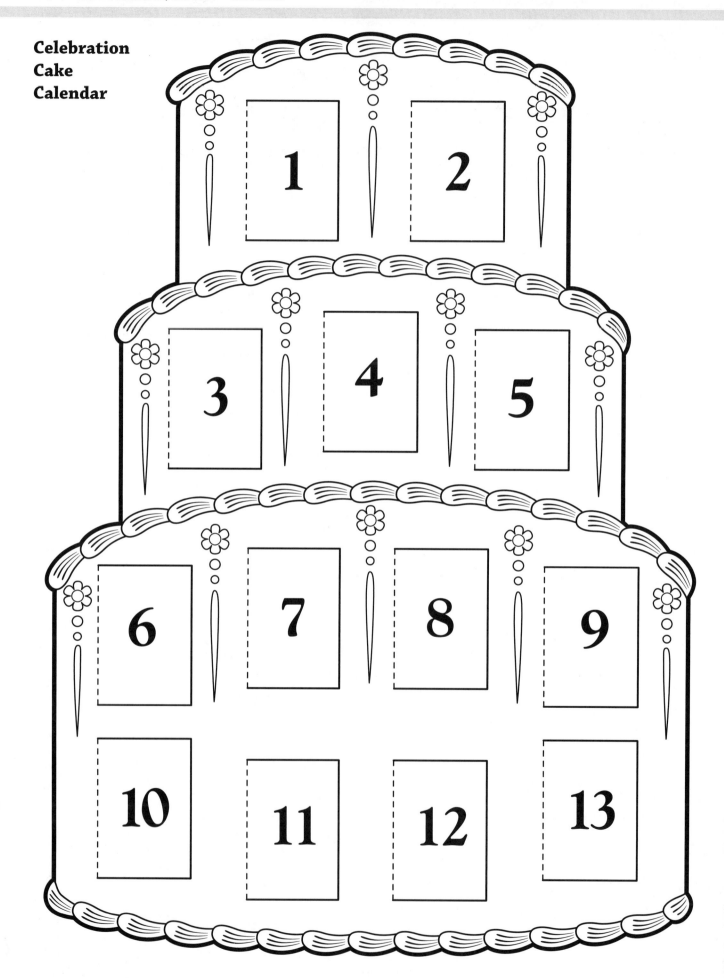

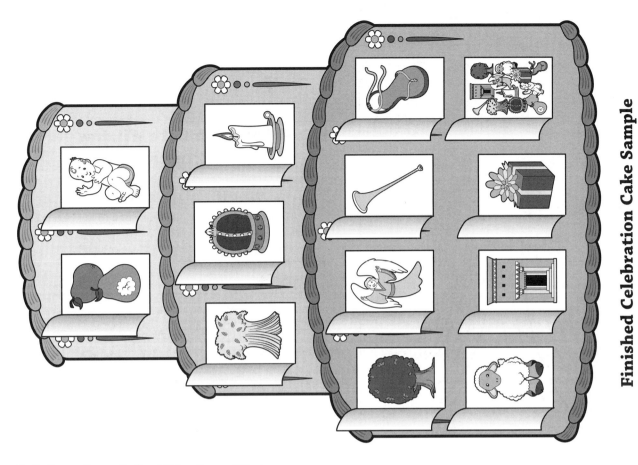

Finished Celebration Cake Sample

Celebration Cake Window Pictures

Door #1

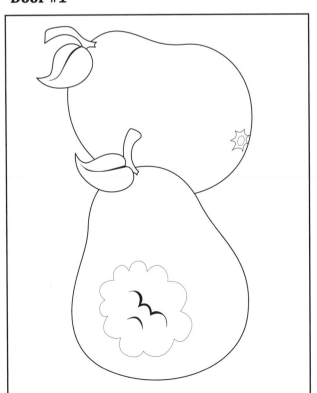

Door #2

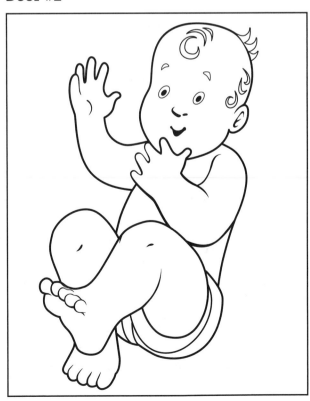

Door #3

Celebration Cake Window
Pictures

Door #4

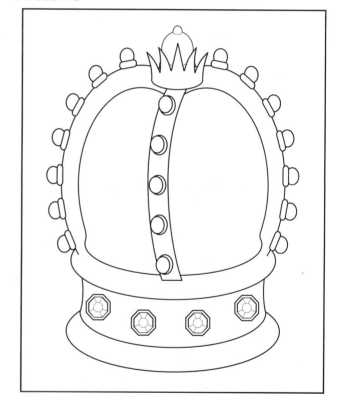

Door #5

Door #6

Door #7

Celebration Cake Window Pictures

Door #8

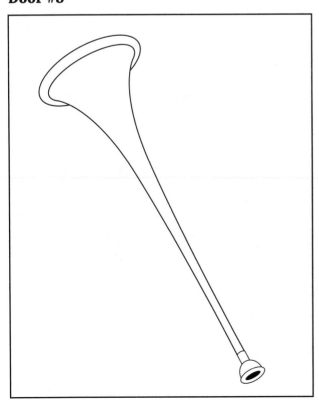

Door #9

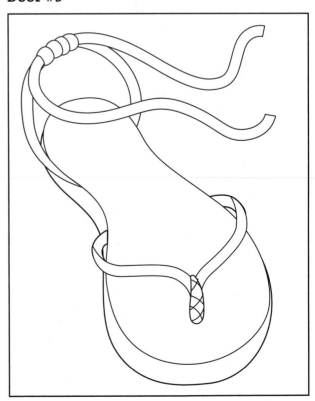

Door #10

Door #11

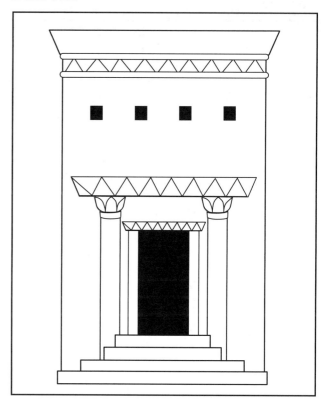

Celebration Cake Window Pictures

Door #12

Door #13

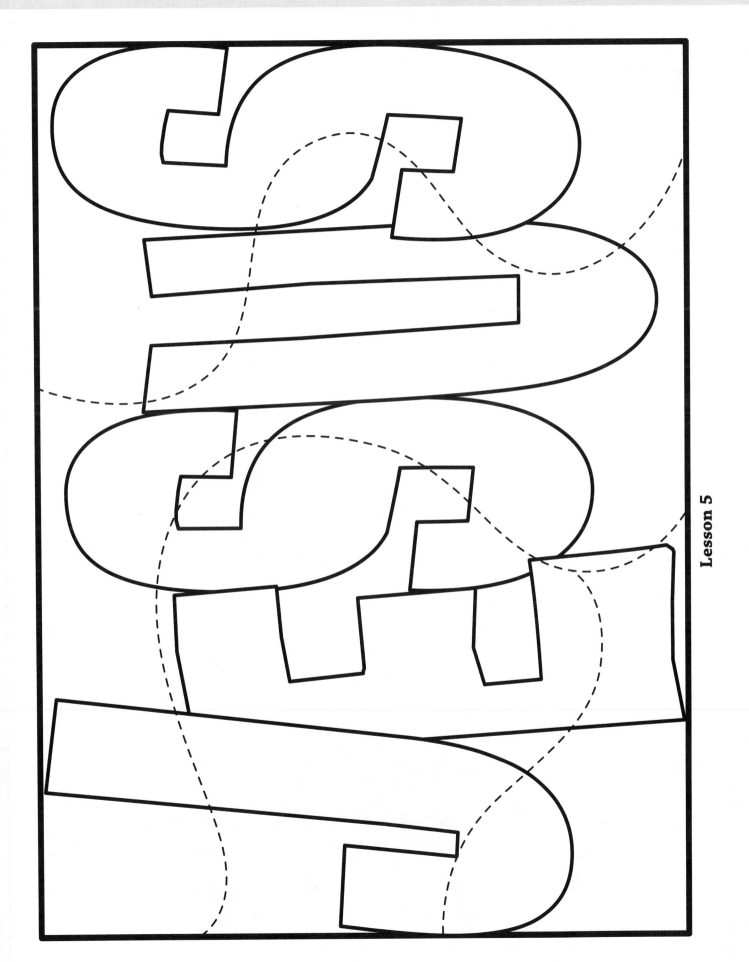

Lesson 5

Family Tree
Lesson 6

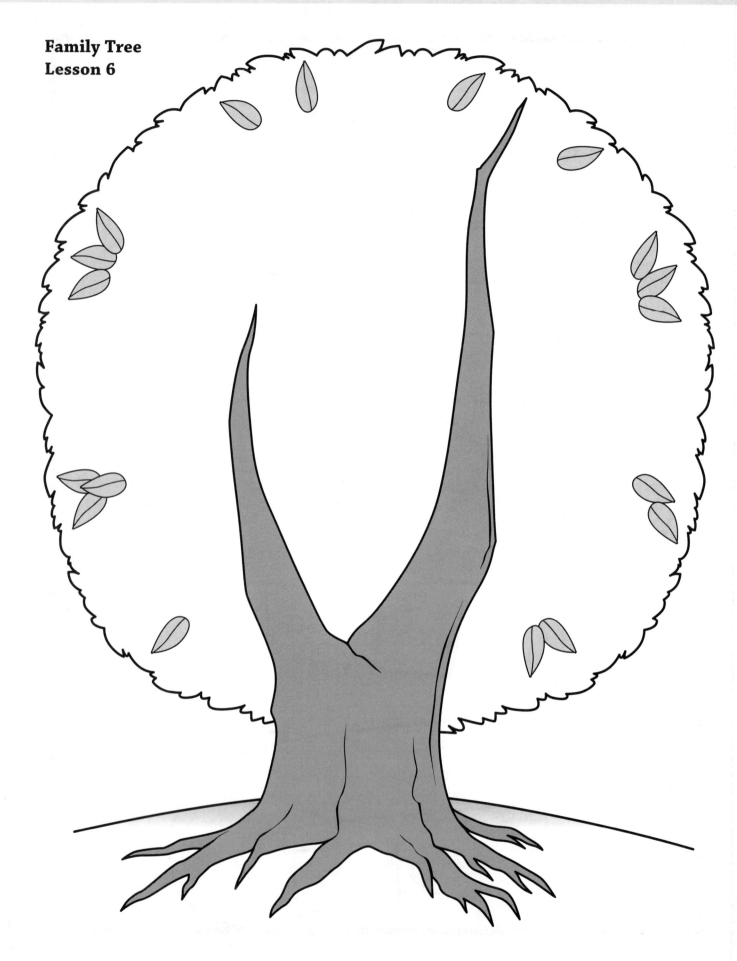

**Angel
Pattern
Lesson 7**

Dear Parents,

Who is Jesus? Why did he come? Over the next 13 weeks, our *Happy Birthday, Jesus!* curriculum will challenge kids to explore God's promise of a Messiah through the Old Testament, and celebrate when that promise comes true in the person of Jesus.

During each lesson, kids will experience a new step in God's plan to bring a Savior to earth by opening another door of the Celebration Calendar, a cake-shaped countdown to Jesus' birth. Your child will experience the excitement of seeing how God fulfilled his promise to save mankind from their sin by sending his only Son to the world.

Every week, your child willl receive an *On the Fast Track!* take-home paper with activities designed to reinforce the Bible truth for that lesson. Papers will include a Bible memory verse, a prayer challenge for parents and kids to do together, and a fun activity for kids to complete. Encourage your child to finish these three activities and bring the signed *Fast Track!* Ticket the following week for a prize.

Our small group prayer times will give children an opportunity to build lifetime habits of prayer. *Happy Birthday, Jesus!* uses the **imPACT** model of prayer to help kids understand the four important activities of prayer—praise, ask, confess, and give thanks. Here are some discussion questions you can use at home to reinforce your child's growing desire to talk with God:

■ *Praise*. Ask your child: **What do you really like about God? Listen to the responses. Let's tell God we like these things about him.** Encourage your child to tell God about these things.

■ *Ask*. It is important for children to know that God cares about their needs. Say: **We can ask God to help us, our families, and our friends with any problems. What would you like to ask God?** Let your child name some prayer requests, then take turns praying for these needs.

■ *Confess*. Tell your child that we all do things we wish we didn't do. Sometimes our actions or words hurt someone and then we are sorry. Ask: **What's one thing you wish you didn't do this last week?** Listen to the response, then, together, bow heads and confess this sin before God.

■ *Give thanks*. Ask: **What are some things that you're thankful that God has done for you or has given to you?** Listen to the responses. Then say: **Let's tell God thank you for these things.** Take turns thanking God.

If you have any questions about this study, please feel free to discuss them with the children's ministry leaders. We are excited about what God is going to do in the lives of our children. We would appreciate your prayers for the teachers and children.

In His Name,

Children's Ministry Coordinator

Dear StationMaster,

Welcome to *Discipleship Junction!* During the next 13 weeks, you will play a major role in the lives of children as you teach them to look for God in every circumstance of life and pray with them in small groups. Our *Happy Birthday, Jesus!* curriculum will help you build habits of prayer into their lives that will last a lifetime.

The **imPACT** model of prayer will remind children about the four important activities of prayer: praise, ask, confess, and give thanks.

■ *Praise. Ask:* **What do you really like about God?** Let volunteers briefly respond, then say: **Let's tell God we like these things about him.** Help children talk to God directly.

■ *Ask.* Ask children: **What would you like to ask God?** Allow children to give prayer requests, then say: **Let's tell God about these needs.** It is important for children to know that God cares about everyone's needs. Have them take turns praying for the needs in their lives.

■ *Confess.* We all do things we wish we didn't do. Sometimes our actions or words hurt someone and then we are sorry. Ask them: **What's one thing that you wish you didn't do this last week?** Give children time to answer, then say: **Let's confess our sins to God and tell him we're sorry.**

■ *Give thanks.* When giving thanks, ask your group: **Tell one thing that you're thankful that God has done for you.** Let children share, then say: **Let's tell God thank you for these things.**

The children's ministry appreciates the important role that you have volunteered to fill. We are confident that God is going to do amazing things in the lives of our children.

Sincerely,

Children's Ministry Coordinator

StationMaster Card #1

This week children learned from Genesis 1—3 that *every person needs a Savior.* They learned how God made a plan to free Adam and Eve and every other person from their sins. Lead your group in prayer using the following four activities:

■ *Praise.* **God made a beautiful world for Adam and Eve.** Prompt students to praise God for specific aspects of creation such as a type of animal, flowers, mountains, or the sun.

■ *Ask.* **God provided all the food and care Adam and Eve needed. What need do you want to ask God for today?**

■ *Confess.* **After Adam and Eve disobeyed God,** **they couldn't be good friends again with God until they asked forgiveness.** Guide students in considering sins they need to confess, and give them time to do so.

■ *Thank.* **When we're truly sorry for what we've done wrong, God is ready to forgive us. Isn't that wonderful? Let's thank God for loving us so much he will forgive us.**

Remember that no child should be forced to pray, but do encourage and invite each one to join you. After praying, talk quietly with the children in your group until the next activity.

StationMaster Card #2

This week your group heard from Genesis 17 and 21 that *God promises Abraham the Savior would come from his family.* They learned how God made a covenant with Abraham and God's promise of a Savior began when Isaac was born. Lead your group in prayer using the following four activities:

■ *Praise.* **God made a covenant with Abraham and kept it.** Allow students to praise God for always keeping his promises.

■ *Ask.* **God asked Abraham to follow him, even though others around him believed in false gods. People today believe in many other things besides the one true God.** Lead students in asking God to make them strong in their desire to follow only him all their lives.

■ *Confess.* **Do you remember how Abraham** laughed when God promised he would have a son, even though he was really old? We all sometimes forget that God can do anything. Think of a time you haven't trusted God to do what might seem impossible, and tell him you're sorry for that.

■ *Thank.* **God sent the Savior he promised, even though it took a long time to happen.** Have students thank God for keeping every one of his promises, including his promise to send Jesus. Children can be thankful in a general way or for specific instances.

Remember that no child should be forced to pray, but do encourage and invite each one to join you. After praying, talk quietly with the children in your group until the next activity.

StationMaster Card #3

This week your group learned from the book of Ruth that *we can trust God to do what is best.* They heard how Ruth followed God and trusted him, and later became a part of the Savior's family. Lead your group in prayer using the following four activities:

■ *Praise.* **God took care of Ruth and Naomi in a famine, when their husbands died, and when they needed food later on. How has he taken care of you?** Model for students how to praise God for his provision and care.

■ *Ask.* **When we trust God but don't know what the right thing to do is, we only have to ask him.** Lead students in asking God for direction or help in their individual situations.

■ *Confess.* **We all have times when we wonder if God will do what he says. Ruth might have doubted too.** Allow children time to ask God's forgiveness for doubting he is God and can do what He promises.

■ *Thank.* **Let's thank God that we can trust him. Thank him for something he has done through you for his glory this week.** Lead children in giving thanks.

Remember that no child should be forced to pray, but do encourage and invite each one to join you. After praying, talk quietly with the children in your group until the next activity.

StationMaster Card #4

This week your group learned from 1 and 2 Samuel that *the Savior comes from a royal family.* They discovered that David became king and that Jesus would come from his family. Lead your group in prayer using the following four activities:

■ *Praise.* **God knew the best man to be king, because he knows all about everyone. No matter what other people see, God sees what's on the inside. Let's praise him for that.**

■ *Ask.* **David was called a man after God's own heart. He wanted to be more like God and follow him closely. Do you want that?** Let children ask God to work in their lives and teach them to follow him.

■ *Confess.* **We often judge people by how they dress or what we see on the outside. Those things don't really show what a person is like inside.** Give time for students to confess when they've judged someone wrongly based on his/her appearance.

■ *Thank.* **Just like God chose David, he has a plan for you and me. Let's thank him for giving us special abilities and having a plan for our lives.** Lead students in thanking God for specific aspects of their personalities.

Remember that no child should be forced to pray, but do encourage and invite each one to join you. After praying, talk quietly with the children in your group until the next activity.

StationMaster Card #5

This week your group learned from Isaiah 7, 9, 11 and Micah 5 that *prophets describe the Messiah— it's Jesus!* They found out how Isaiah and Micah prophesied who Jesus would be, and how God's promises about the Messiah would be fulfilled when Jesus was born. Lead your group in prayer using the following four activities:

■ *Praise.* **God told his people about Jesus for centuries before Jesus actually came.** Have students praise God for knowing what's happening now and what will happen in the future.

■ *Ask.* **Most people didn't recognize Jesus when he came.** Have students ask God to open their eyes to all that he is doing in their lives and the world.

■ *Confess.* **Jesus came to make us free from our sins. Right now you can tell God you're sorry for sins you know you've done. He'll be glad to forgive you.**

■ *Thank.* **What other promises has God made that he has kept?** Lead the children in thanking God for specific promises he has fulfilled.

Remember that no child should be forced to pray, but do encourage and invite each one to join you. After praying, talk quietly with the children in your group until the next activity.

StationMaster Card #6

This week your group learned from Luke 3 that *people waited a long time for the Savior*. They learned that Jesus' family tree went all the way back to Adam and included some Bible people they've heard about. Lead your group in prayer using the following four activities:

- *Praise.* **God chose just the right time to send Jesus.** Help students praise God for knowing the right time for everything.
- *Ask.* **Many people lived and died waiting for the Messiah. What are you waiting for from God? This is a good time to pray and trust God for the things you need.**
- *Confess.* **We can get impatient waiting for God to answer our prayers like we want him to.** Challenge students to think about their prayers and what they think about God when he doesn't do what they ask. Lead them in confessing wrong reasons for their prayers or lack of trust that God will answer.
- *Thank.* **God knows the right time for all the things you're waiting for, too.** Have students thank God for being patient even when they are not.

Remember that no child should be forced to pray, but do encourage and invite each one to join you. After praying, talk quietly with the children in your group until the next activity.

StationMaster Card #7

This week your group learned from Matthew 1 and Luke 1 that *God announces his Son is coming*. They heard how an angel told Mary and Joseph about the Messiah. Lead your group in prayer using the following four activities:

- *Praise.* **God used an angel to tell Mary she would have a baby. He told her nothing was impossible with God.** Lead students in praising God for doing even what seems impossible.
- *Ask.* **God sent his messages to Mary and Joseph through an angel. He probably won't talk to us using an angel, but he does want to talk to us.** Students can ask God to help them hear him better every day.
- *Confess.* **Remember how Mary accepted the angel's message even though it wasn't what she had planned for her life? It can be hard to accept God's words for our life.** Have children confess times that they have not paid attention to what God wanted for them and went their own ways instead.
- *Thank.* **Let's thank God that Mary and Joseph were willing to be Jesus' parents.** Encourage children to give thanks to God for answered prayer as well.

Remember that no child should be forced to pray, but do encourage and invite each one to join you. After praying, talk quietly with the children in your group until the next activity.

StationMaster Card #8

This week your group learned from Malachi 3 that *John the Baptist prepares the way for Jesus.* They learned how John was God's last messenger before Jesus came. Lead your group in prayer using the following four activities:

■ *Praise.* **God sent John so that as many people as possible would recognize Jesus, the Messiah.** Have students praise God for caring so much about people.

■ *Ask.* **John told people to repent, or be sorry for their sin, and change their ways. God wants us to do that too.** Give children a chance to ask God to show them their sins.

■ *Confess.* **If God has shown you some sins in your life, you can get them cleaned up right now. Tell him you're sorry for disobeying him and doing wrong. He's glad to forgive you.**

■ *Thank.* **John was the last prophet before the Messiah came to die for our sins.** Students can thank God for having such a huge love for them that he carried out his plan of salvation.

Remember that no child should be forced to pray, but do encourage and invite each one to join you. After praying, talk quietly with the children in your group until the next activity.

StationMaster Card #9

This week your group learned from Micah 5 and Luke 2 that *God chose Bethlehem to be Jesus' birthplace.* They found out how God caused circumstances to happen so Jesus would be born in Bethlehem. Lead your group in prayer using the following four activities:

■ *Praise.* **God was able to get the most powerful leader of the day to take a census so Mary and Joseph would go to Bethlehem.** Lead students in praising God for having the power to work everything out to accomplish his plans.

■ *Ask.* **Mary and Joseph had to walk 70 miles to travel from Nazareth to Bethlehem. That was hard! But God helped them.** Children can ask God for help with things that seem hard to them.

■ *Confess.* **Herod tried to go against God's plan. We don't always want to do things God's way either.** Give children time to confess their wrong choices and times of wanting to do things their way instead of God's.

■ *Thank.* **Just like God planned exactly how Jesus' birth would work out, he's planned how your life will work out. When you choose to live God's way, he has the best plan for you.** Lead children in thanking God for overseeing their lives in every way.

Remember that no child should be forced to pray, but do encourage and invite each one to join you. After praying, talk quietly with the children in your group until the next activity.

StationMaster Card #10

This week your group learned from Luke 2 that the *angels invite the shepherds to worship Jesus*. They learned that they can worship Jesus just like the shepherds did. Lead your group in prayer using the following four activities:

- *Praise.* **God honored the shepherds in the field no matter how dirty or poor they might have been.** Guide children in giving praise to God for seeing all people equally.
- *Ask.* **The angels invited the shepherds to Bethlehem to see baby Jesus. We can ask God for chances to see Jesus in our lives every day. Let's do that now.**
- *Confess.* **We don't always want to worship God or give him the honor he deserves. Let God show you any times you haven't honored him like you need to. Then ask for his forgiveness.**
- *Thank.* **We can worship God any time and in any way. People in some countries don't have that choice.** Lead children in thanksgiving for freedom to worship.

Remember that no child should be forced to pray, but do encourage and invite each one to join you. After praying, talk quietly with the children in your group until the next activity.

StationMaster Card #11

This week your group learned from Luke 2 that *the righteous recognize and honor Jesus*. They discovered that Simeon and Anna praised God for being able to see the Messiah before they died. Lead your group in prayer using the following four activities:

- *Praise.* **Simeon recognized Jesus at the temple because he was led by the Holy Spirit.** Have students praise God for speaking to people through his Holy Spirit.
- *Ask.* **Simeon recognized Jesus when he saw the baby. Would you recognize God's presence in your day? Ask God to open the eyes of your spirit so you can see him in every day.**
- *Confess.* **We sometimes don't pay attention when God is with us. The last time you were scared or nervous or worshipping in church, did you pay attention to God? Let's let God know we're sorry for times we ignore him.**
- *Thank.* **Simeon and Anna were godly older people who had strong faith in the Lord.** Give students opportunity to thank God for older people who are godly examples to them.

Remember that no child should be forced to pray, but do encourage and invite each one to join you. After praying, talk quietly with the children in your group until the next activity.

StationMaster Card #12

This week your group learned from Matthew 2 that *wise men worship Jesus*. They learned how the magi stopped to ask Herod for directions. Lead your group in prayer using the following four activities:

- *Praise.* **God put a star in the sky to lead the wise men to Jesus.** Have students praise God for using his creation to bring people to him.
- *Ask.* **When the wise men got to Jerusalem they stopped and asked for directions.** Have students ask God for his directions concerning their lives.

- *Confess.* **Herod lied to the wise men when he said he wanted to worship Jesus.** Have students ask God for forgiveness for any lies they know they have told.
- *Thank.* **God warned the wise men about Herod.** Have students thank God for always being in control.

Remember that no child should be forced to pray, but do encourage and invite each one to join you. After praying, talk quietly with the children in your group until the next activity.

StationMaster Card #13

This week your group learned from Luke 2 that *God keeps his promise*. They learned how Jesus was born as a baby, but that he was also with God when the world was created. Lead your group in prayer using the following four activities:

- *Praise.* **One of Jesus' names is Light of the World. He gives light to our hearts.** Lead students in praise to God that Jesus is light, and no darkness can extinguish his light.
- *Ask.* **We might ask for toys and games for Christmas, but God is so delighted when we ask him to teach us to be more like his Son.** Guide children in praying for God to make them more like Jesus.

- *Confess.* **It's sometimes easy to forget what Christmas is really about. It's not about special candy and gifts and parties. It's really about Jesus. Let's each tell God we're sorry for being selfish at Christmas and forgetting whose birthday it is.**
- *Thank.* **God promised the world a Messiah, and he kept his promise.** Lead children in a prayer of thanksgiving that God does exactly what he says he will do.

Remember that no child should be forced to pray, but do encourage and invite each one to join you. After praying, talk quietly with the children in your group until the next activity.

On the Fast Track!

Prayer Challenge

With someone at home: Walk around your block or go to a park with your family. Collect some of nature: leaves, pinecones, sticks, rocks, etc. Bring them home and praise God for making such wonderful things. Thank him for the things in nature you like the most.

Bible Memory Verse

I am not ashamed of the gospel, because it is the power of God for the salvation of everyone who believes **(Romans 1:16).**

*Early elementary verse in **bold** type.*

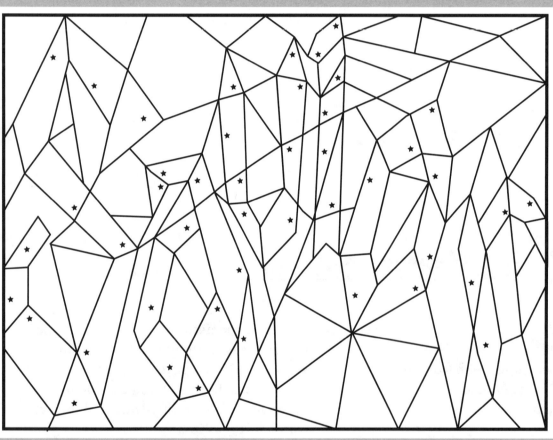

Hidden Word Picture

Color in the sections that have a star. When you're finished, you'll be able to fill in the missing word in this sentence: Every person needs a _____.

Dear Parents and Guardians,

Please check off the items your child completed this week:

- ☐ Prayer Challenge
- ☐ Memory Verse
- ☐ Think and Do
- ☐ Hidden Word Picture

Adult Signature:

_____

FAST TRACK! TICKET

Think and Do

Create a drawing or painting of a tree with leaves and fruit using your favorite art materials. Add Adam and Eve and yourself near the tree. Tell someone in your family the story you heard in class about Adam and Eve in the Garden of Eden.

Word Search

Find the names from the Bible story:
- Abraham
- Sarah
- Isaac
- covenant
- laugh
- impossible
- promise
- Savior

P	C	O	V	C	L	I	G	H
R	L	A	U	G	H	M	P	C
O	U	B	M	S	G	P	S	O
M	N	T	S	V	A	O	A	V
I	S	A	A	C	F	S	B	E
S	A	F	R	G	R	S	R	N
E	V	R	A	R	D	I	A	A
N	I	S	H	N	M	B	H	N
V	O	E	T	E	S	L	A	T
S	R	A	V	I	L	E	M	D

Prayer Challenge

At least two times this week, talk to God by praising him for doing what seems impossible to us. Each time, name one thing he's done that is impossible for people.

Think and Do

Count on a calendar how many days it is until Christmas. That's the day we celebrate Jesus coming to earth to be our Savior. Make a paper Christmas ornament or Christmas card and put it in your room. When you see it, you'll remember that even though it's a long time until Christmas, you know it's coming. It will also remind you that God promised to send a Savior—and he did!

Bible Memory Verse

And we have seen and testify that **the Father has sent his Son to be the Savior of the world** (1 John 4:14).

*Early elementary verse in **bold** type.*

Dear Parents and Guardians,

Please check off the items your child completed this week:

❏ Prayer Challenge
❏ Memory Verse
❏ Think and Do
❏ Word Search

Adult Signature: _____

FAST TRACK! TICKET

On the Fast Track!

Prayer Challenge

Ruth had a character that pleased God. She cared about others, worked hard, trusted God to do what is best, and followed wise advice from older Christians. Ask God to show you how to have a character that pleases him.

Bible Memory Verse

When Jesus spoke again to the people, he said, **"I am the light of the world. Whoever follows me will never walk in darkness,** but will have the light of life" (John 8:12).

*Early elementary verse in **bold** type.*

Grain Prayer Reminder

On a separate sheet of paper, write the words "I am the light of the world" in large letters. Then glue kernels of barley, corn, or rice in interesting patterns on top of the letters. Display this in your room as a reminder to pray and ask God to help you be "light" at home and school.

Think and Do

Ruth was a hardworking woman who served Naomi. She's the kind of example God wants us to follow. Find a way to serve this week and work hard at it. You can serve people at home, at school, in your neighborhood, at church, or another place. When you see your teacher next week, share how you served.

Dear Parents and Guardians,
Please check off the items your child completed this week:

❑ Prayer Challenge
❑ Memory Verse
❑ Think and Do
❑ Grain Prayer Reminder

Adult Signature: _____

FAST TRACK! TICKET

Prayer Challenge

Even though you probably won't be chosen to be a king or queen, what's in your heart is very important to God. And there's always room to become more like him. This week, pray with an adult at home for God to work in your heart to be someone who pleases him.

Bible Memory Verse

The Lord does not look at the things man looks at. **Man looks at the outward appearance, but the LORD looks at the heart** (1 Samuel 16:7).

Early elementary verse in **bold** *type.*

Scrambled Words

Unscramble these words about this week's Bible story. If you are just learning to read, ask an older person to help you figure out the first letter.

nikg ___ ___ ___ ___

treah ___ ___ ___ ___ ___

vaDdi ___ ___ ___ ___ ___

hepes ___ ___ ___ ___ ___

sseuJ ___ ___ ___ ___ ___

Think and Do

When God looks at our hearts, what does he want to see? Make a large red heart and draw or write in it the kinds of things God wants to find in our hearts, like sharing and serving. Show the heart to your mom or dad, then put it where it will remind you to keep asking God for these qualities.

Dear Parents and Guardians,
Please check off the items your child completed this week:

- ❏ Prayer Challenge
- ❏ Memory Verse
- ❏ Think and Do
- ❏ Scrambled Words

Adult Signature: _____

FAST TRACK! TICKET

On the Fast Track!

Prayer Challenge

We all need a Savior because we've all disobeyed God and made wrong choices. God wants to forgive every sin when we tell him we're sorry. Every day (like before you go to sleep), confess your wrongs to Jesus. Tell him you're sorry for those things, and thank him for always forgiving you.

Bible Memory Verse

I am the LORD, your God, the Holy One of Israel, your Savior (Isaiah 43:3).

Messiah Acrostic Poem

Make an acrostic poem using the letters in the word "Messiah." Next to each letter, write a word or sentence that starts with that letter or sound. The word or sentence should be about Jesus. The first letter is done for you.

My sins are forgiven. _____

E _____

S _____

S _____

I _____

A _____

H _____

Think and Do

God promised his people a Savior and he kept his promise. This week, make a small promise to someone and keep it. Tell someone at home about your experience and how it made you feel.

Dear Parents and Guardians,
Please check off the items your child completed this week:

❑ Prayer Challenge
❑ Memory Verse
❑ Think and Do
❑ Messiah Acrostic Poem

Adult Signature: _____

FAST TRACK! TICKET

On the Fast Track!

Prayer Challenge

Patience helps us wait for things that take a long time to happen. This week, ask God for patience about things you must wait for. Ask him to remind you to be patient when you wait in line at school, wait for a ride, or wait for someone to help you. Thank him at the end of the week for the ways you've had to use patience.

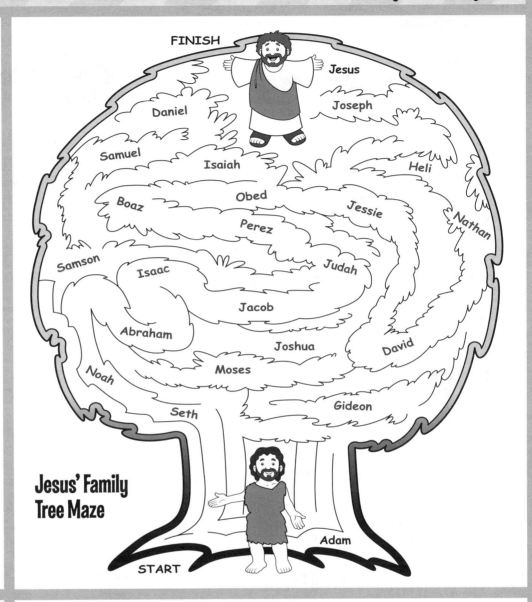

FINISH

Jesus

Joseph

Daniel

Heli

Samuel

Isaiah

Nathan

Boaz

Obed

Jessie

Perez

Samson

Judah

Isaac

Jacob

Abraham

Joshua

David

Moses

Noah

Gideon

Seth

Adam

Jesus' Family Tree Maze

START

Bible Memory Verse

Wait for the LORD; be strong and take heart and wait for the LORD (Psalm 27:14).

Think and Do

Ask someone at home to help you make your own family tree with your parents, brothers and sisters, and grandparents on it. Go back as far as you can.

Dear Parents and Guardians,
Please check off the items your child completed this week:

❑ Prayer Challenge
❑ Memory Verse
❑ Think and Do
❑ Jesus' Family Tree Maze

Adult Signature: _____

FAST TRACK! TICKET

On the Fast Track!

Prayer Challenge

Wouldn't it be amazing if an angel came to talk to you like Gabriel did to Mary and Joseph? Every day this week, pray God would open your spiritual ears so you will hear him however he chooses to speak to you.

Bible Memory Verse

This is love: not that we loved God, but that he loved us and sent his Son as an atoning sacrifice for our sins **(1 John 4:10)**.

*Early elementary verse in **bold** type.*

Think and Do

Do this experiment with your parents: Place a clear cup of water on the table, and mix in a tablespoon of salt. Put in a raw egg. Does it float? If not, add another tablespoon of salt. Continue until the egg floats. Wow! Although a floating egg seems impossible, there are scientific elements that cause it to float and appear to do the impossible. God doesn't need science to do the impossible. He can do anything!

Discover the Message

Uncover the words that were in the angel's message to Mary. Starting with the first letter, cross out every other letter. Then write the letters that are left on the line. It's a really important part of the angel's message, and it's true.

MJoelssups _____

nits _____

ytvhJe _____

dSbotn _____

hoLf _____

SGroed _____

Dear Parents and Guardians,
Please check off the items your child completed this week:

❑ Prayer Challenge
❑ Memory Verse
❑ Think and Do
❑ Discover the Message

Adult Signature: _____

FAST TRACK! TICKET

On the Fast Track!

Prayer Challenge

When you pray this week, prepare your heart to see and hear from God by praying your memory verse. If you can't read yet, ask an older person to pray with you and they can read it. Then be quiet for a little while to give God time to show you anything you need to tell him or ask forgiveness for.

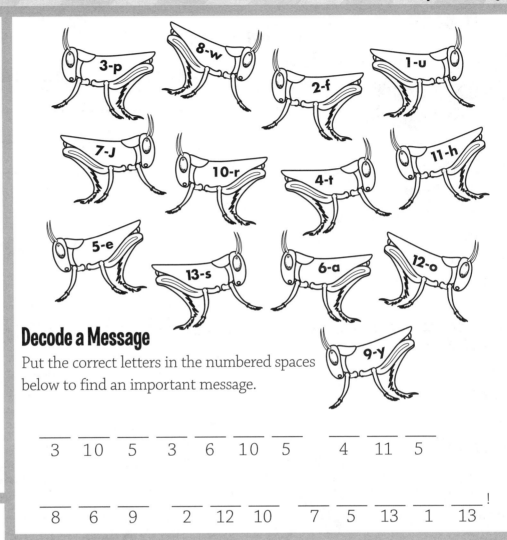

Decode a Message

Put the correct letters in the numbered spaces below to find an important message.

___ ___ ___ ___ ___ ___ ___ ___ ___ ___
3 10 5 3 6 10 5   4 11 5

___ ___ ___ ___ ___ ___ ___ ___ ___ ___ ___!
8 6 9   2 12 10   7 5 13 1 13

Bible Memory Verse

Test me, O LORD, and try me, **examine my heart and my mind; for your love is ever before me,** and I walk continually in your truth **(Psalm 26:2-3).**

*Early Elementary verse in **bold** type.*

Think and Do

Prepare the way for Jesus in your neighborhood. Make a poster or sign with a message that tells the reason Jesus came, like: "Jesus loves you" or "Jesus came to give us life." Add some color to it, then put your sign or poster on your front door. Get permission from a parent or adult if you need to before hanging up your sign.

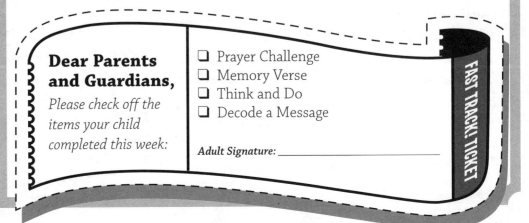

Dear Parents and Guardians,
Please check off the items your child completed this week:

❏ Prayer Challenge
❏ Memory Verse
❏ Think and Do
❏ Decode a Message

Adult Signature: _____

FAST TRACK! TICKET

On the Fast Track!

Prayer Challenge

God is powerful and capable of making things work out for the best. This week, tell God you want to follow his directions so you can enjoy your life the way he wants you to.

Think and Do

Your memory verse this week is so helpful to people who are going through a hard time. Find someone—with an adult's help if needed—who is going through a sad or hard time. Think of a way you can encourage that person, and make sharing your verse part of your encouragement. It might be an e-mail, a card, or a drawing. You decide.

Crossword Puzzle

Fill in the puzzle using the clues below.

9. Herod asked the high _____ and teachers where the Messiah would be born.
10. He was engaged to marry Mary.

Across:
2. How Mary and Joseph traveled to Bethlehem.
4. _____ Augustus wanted to count the people in his land.
5. Mary and Joseph traveled 70 _____ to Bethlehem.
6. A kind of grain.
7. Jesus is the _____ of God.

Down:
1. The mother of Jesus
2. Swaddling clothes kept baby Jesus _____.
3. Whoever believes in Jesus and will have _____ life (John 3:16).
4. An official count of all the people.
8. The king who wanted to know where Jesus would be born.

Bible Memory Verse

The LORD himself goes before you and will be with you; he will never leave you nor forsake you. Do not be afraid; do not be discouraged **(Deuteronomy 31:8).**

*Early elementary verse in **bold** type.*

Dear Parents and Guardians,
Please check off the items your child completed this week:

- ☐ Prayer Challenge
- ☐ Memory Verse
- ☐ Think and Do
- ☐ Crossword Puzzle

Adult Signature: _____

FAST TRACK! TICKET

On the Fast Track!

Think and Do

Follow the angels' example in the Bible story and tell about Jesus to someone you know. You can ask a school friend or teammate over to watch a Christian DVD, read a Christian book together, or you can even take your friend to church with you. Be sure you tell your friend the reason you invited him or her: to meet Jesus!

Decode the Answer

What did the shepherds decide after the angels visited them? Decode the answer by writing the letter from the code on the line.

Code:

1	2	3	4	5	6	7	8	9	10	11	12	13
A	B	C	D	E	F	G	H	I	J	K	L	M

14	15	16	17	18	19	20	21	22	23	24	25	26
N	O	P	Q	R	S	T	U	V	W	X	Y	Z

___ ___ ___ ___ ' ___ ___ ___ ___ ___ ___ ___ ___ ___ ___ ___
12 5 20 19   7 15   20 15   2 5 20 8 12 5 8 5 13

___ ___ ___ ___ ___ ___ ___ ___ ___ ___ ___ ___ ___ ___ ___
1 14 4   19 5 5   20 8 9 19   20 8 9 14 7

___ ___ ___ ___ ___ ___ ___ ___ ___ ___ ___ ___ ___ ___ ___ '
20 8 1 20   8 1 19   8 1 16 16 5 14 5 4

___ ___ ___ ___ ___ ___ ___ ___ ___ ___ ___ ___ ___ ___ ___
23 8 9 3 8   20 8 5   12 15 18 4   20 15 12 4

___ ___ ___ ___ ___ ___ ." ___ ___ ___ ___ 2:15 ___
21 19   1 2 15 21 20   12 21 11 5   2

Prayer Challenge

Think how excited the angels must have been that the Messiah was born! They had been waiting centuries to announce his birth. Each day when you pray this week, praise God for his great plan and for sharing it with you.

Bible Memory Verse

You make me glad by your deeds,
O LORD; I sing for joy at the works of your hands
(Psalm 92:4).

Dear Parents and Guardians,

Please check off the items your child completed this week:

❑ Prayer Challenge
❑ Memory Verse
❑ Think and Do
❑ Decode the Answer

Adult Signature: _____

FAST TRACK! TICKET

On the Fast Track!

Prayer Challenge

To be righteous like Simeon and Anna, love God with all your heart and do what is right. Ask your parents to pray with you that every day you will grow to love God with all your heart, mind, and strength. Praise God for loving you more than you can imagine.

Righteous or Unrighteous

Draw a happy or sad face to show which things are right before God and which are not right.

○ 1. I get angry when I don't get my own way.

○ 2. I obey my parents.

○ 3. I do my homework on time.

○ 4. I do my chores before I'm told.

○ 5. I talk to Jesus every day.

○ 6. If I don't do my chores, I lie about it.

○ 7. I laugh when someone makes fun of another person.

○ 8. I tell others about how great Jesus is.

○ 9. I take things that don't belong to me.

○ 10. I read my Bible.

Think and Do

Ask a godly older person (at church, in your family) to tell you about how he or she got to know Jesus. Ask that person to pray for you this week so you can be more like Jesus.

Bible Memory Verse

The heavens proclaim his righteousness, and all the peoples see his glory (Psalm 97:6).

Dear Parents and Guardians,
Please check off the items your child completed this week:

❑ Prayer Challenge
❑ Memory Verse
❑ Think and Do
❑ Righteous or Unrighteous

Adult Signature: _____

FAST TRACK! TICKET

On the Fast Track!

Think and Do

Besides giving your life to Jesus, you can give him your time and talents. Sometime this week, ask your parents to help you choose a way you can serve Jesus. Some ideas: do some chores for an elderly person, offer your time to your church for an afternoon, help in the church nursery (if you're old enough), or put some of your toys in a garage sale and place the money you earned in the church offering.

Wise Men Maze

Find the path of the wise men to the star.

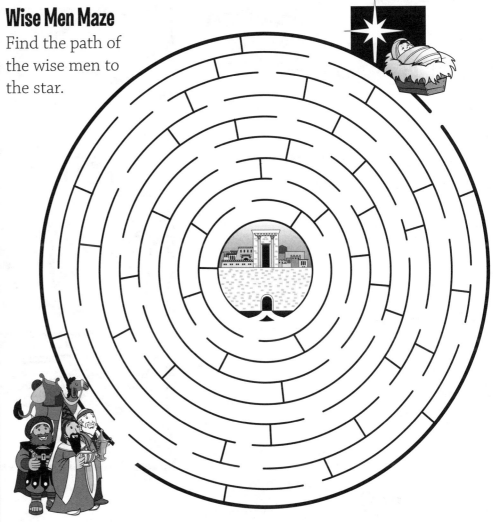

Bible Memory Verse

From infancy you have known **the holy Scriptures,** which **are able to make you wise for salvation through faith in Christ Jesus** (2 Timothy 3:15).

*Early elementary verse in **bold** type.*

Prayer Challenge

This week, ask God for directions. Each day, tell God you want to do things his way and that you want to know his directions. Talk to your parents about what you think God is directing you to do.

Dear Parents and Guardians,

Please check off the items your child completed this week:

- ☐ Prayer Challenge
- ☐ Memory Verse
- ☐ Think and Do
- ☐ Wise Men Maze

Adult Signature: _____

FAST TRACK! TICKET

On the Fast Track!

Prayer Challenge

The Jews prayed for the Messiah to come, and they waited. God answered by sending Jesus. When you pray this week, tell God that you trust him to answer your prayers according to his will, because he is trustworthy and always keeps his promises.

Bible Memory Verse

The Word became flesh and made his dwelling among us. We have seen his glory, the glory of the One and Only, who came from the Father, full of grace and truth **(John 1:14)**.

*Early Elementary verse in **bold** type.*

Hidden Picture

Color the dotted sections to find the hidden picture.

What is the hidden picture?

_____

What does it stand for?

_____

_____

● = yellow   ▲ = red   ■ = blue

Think and Do

With your parents' permission, set up a white candle on your kitchen table or a place where your family gets together. Have a short family time this week and light the candle. Tell your family why this is called the Jesus candle. Sing some Christmas songs that tell about Jesus and his birth.

Dear Parents and Guardians,
Please check off the items your child completed this week:

❑ Prayer Challenge
❑ Memory Verse
❑ Think and Do
❑ Hidden Picture

Adult Signature: _____

FAST TRACK! TICKET